3.4.18

To Alice
With sincere best wishes for your medical and professional future - I have every confidence it's bright! Helena

HELENA McKEOWN

CW01590393

Social Research in Health and Illness

Social Research in Health and Illness offers a theoretically informed guide to practising the key social research methods in investigating health and illness. Examining both methods and methodology, the authors explore the importance of selecting the appropriate research method for the project in question, demonstrating that researchers do not simply apply a set of neutral techniques to the issues that they investigate, but take part in a dynamic, reflective engagement with social and cultural worlds in a process of continual learning.

With its application of a variety of research methods to concrete cases, this book provides a sociology of specific health conditions, thus rendering them more understandable, while clarifying the nature of research concepts, approaches, methods and methodologies by demonstrating their use in real-life settings. Drawing on case studies involving a range of health conditions, including mental illness, HIV, diabetes, kidney disease, Alzheimer's disease, heart disease, breast cancer, thalassaemia and multiple sclerosis, the authors examine a range of methodological issues, exploring the use of focus groups, observation, data archives, interviews and surveys, while also considering questions of ethics and analysis.

A comprehensive and practical examination of research methods in use in a defined field of social scientific enquiry, this volume is essential reading for scholars, graduate students and healthcare professionals with interests in conducting qualitative and quantitative research in the fields of health and medicine.

Constantinos N. Phellas is Professor and Vice Rector for Faculty and Research, University of Nicosia, Cyprus and editor of *Researching Non-Heterosexual Sexualities*.

Costas S. Constantinou is Associate Professor and Lead for Medical Sociology at the University of Nicosia Medical School, Cyprus.

Routledge Advances in Health and Social Policy

For a full list of titles in this series, please visit https://www.routledge.com/Routledge-Advances-in-Health-and-Social-Policy/book-series/RAHSP

Titles in this series:

Social Development and Social Work Perspectives on Social Protection
Edited by Julie Drolet

Social Policies and Public Action
Lavinia Bifulco

Alcohol, Power and Public Health
A Comparative Study of Alcohol Policy
Shane Butler, Betsy Thom, James Nicholls and Karen Elmeland

Planning Later Life
Bioethics and Public Health in Ageing Societies
Edited by Mark Schweda, Larissa Pfaller, Kai Brauer, Frank Adloff & Silke Schicktanz

Moralising Poverty
The 'Undeserving' Poor in the Public Gaze
Serena Romano

The End of Physiotherapy
Critical Physiotherapy for the Twenty-First Century
David Nicholls

Effective Interventions for Unemployed Young People in Europe
Social Innovation or Paradigm Shift?
Edited by Tomas Sirovatka and Henk Spies

Social Research in Health and Illness
Case-Based Approaches
Constantinos N. Phellas and Costas S. Constantinou

Social Research in Health and Illness

Case-Based Approaches

Constantinos N. Phellas and Costas S. Constantinou

Routledge
Taylor & Francis Group
LONDON AND NEW YORK

First published 2018
by Routledge
2 Park Square, Milton Park, Abingdon, Oxon OX14 4RN

and by Routledge
711 Third Avenue, New York, NY 10017

Routledge is an imprint of the Taylor & Francis Group, an informa business

© 2018 Constantinos N. Phellas and Costas S. Constantinou

The right of Constantinos N. Phellas and Costas S. Constantinou to be identified as authors of this work has been asserted by them in accordance with sections 77 and 78 of the Copyright, Designs and Patents Act 1988.

All rights reserved. No part of this book may be reprinted or reproduced or utilised in any form or by any electronic, mechanical, or other means, now known or hereafter invented, including photocopying and recording, or in any information storage or retrieval system, without permission in writing from the publishers.

Trademark notice: Product or corporate names may be trademarks or registered trademarks, and are used only for identification and explanation without intent to infringe.

British Library Cataloguing-in-Publication Data
A catalogue record for this book is available from the British Library

Library of Congress Cataloging in Publication Data
Names: Phellas, Constantinos N., author. | Constantinou, Costas S., author.
Title: Social research in health and illness: case-based approaches / Constantinos N. Phellas and Costas S. Constantinou.
Other titles: Routledge advances in health and social policy.
Description: Abingdon, Oxon; New York, NY: Routledge, 2017. |
Series: Routledge advances in health and social policy |
Includes bibliographical references.
Identifiers: LCCN 2017009516 | ISBN 9781472452283 (hardback) |
ISBN 9781315609607 (ebook)
Subjects: | MESH: Research Design | Health Surveys–methods |
Review Literature as Topic | Ethics, Research
Classification: LCC RA407 | NLM WA 20.5 | DDC 614.4/2–dc23
LC record available at https://lccn.loc.gov/2017009516

ISBN: 978-1-4724-5228-3 (hbk)
ISBN: 978-1-315-60960-7 (ebk)

Typeset in Times New Roman
by Deanta Global Publishing Services, Chennai, India

MIX
Paper from responsible sources
FSC® C013056

Printed and bound in Great Britain by
TJ International Ltd, Padstow, Cornwall

Contents

Foreword

I would like to congratulate the authors on providing a very insightful and practical book for those interested in conducting empirical research to investigate health and illness in human populations. The Introduction presents the philosophical grounds of quantitative and qualitative research, while each chapter unfolds with a case study to capture the medical focus of the text that follows in order to enable the reader to identify with a real-life scenario. Each case is theoretically informed and adopts an appropriate methodological strategy to carefully address specific research questions. A strong applied thread runs through the suitability of each methodological approach that is adopted to tackle each real-life scenario.

The book begins with how to do a literature review and concludes with a final chapter on ethics. These important chapters "top and tail" nine interwoven expositions of the following applications: the social survey, qualitative interviewing, the focus group, ethnographic observation, coding and analysis, Internet research, and the value of combining both quantitative and qualitative methods, concluding with use of existing data. The authors succeed in presenting the reader with a rich source of further reading for new and existing health researchers to reflect upon the application of each method. The book will appeal to health research trainers, their students and a wider constituency of health professionals who are interested in the business of doing research in the context of health and illness.

Professor Richard D. Wiggins
UCL Institute of Education, London, UK

Introduction

Research relates to ways of understanding reality. There are two important questions to consider here: "what" and "how" to know about this reality. What to know relates to ontological approaches, such as realism and idealism (Ormston *et al.*, 2014). According to realism, reality exists outside individuals and is independent of an individual's thoughts and actions. Therefore, reality can be identified and measured with the help of a set of tools. Idealism refers to the process of creating reality through human interaction. Reality, therefore, according to idealism, does not exist outside individuals and cannot be understood without them. The question of how to know about reality is addressed by epistemology. Deduction and induction pertain to epistemological procedural ways of understanding reality and relate to the ontologies of realism and idealism. More specifically, deduction refers to a process whereby a researcher starts with a theory or a hypothesis and then conducts research in order to test this hypothesis. The process of induction follows a different path. That is, a researcher collects and analyses data in order to construct a theory or a model (Bowling, 2014). Deduction reflects the philosophical tenets of realism, and induction reflects those of idealism. From this philosophical and procedural pairing, two main theories accrued (Crotty, 1998): (1) positivism, which aligns with realism and deduction, aiming to discover laws that cause phenomena to happen, and (2) interpretivism (based on idealism and induction), which focuses on how individuals make sense of their world.

The theoretical frameworks of positivism and interpretivism created two traditions in research: quantitative research and qualitative research. Quantitative research relies heavily on realism and positivism and follows a deductive approach, whereas qualitative research draws from realism and interpretivism and is largely inductive. Therefore, these two traditions had to collect different types of data in order to align with their theoretical and foundational grounds. More specifically, quantitative research aims to measure phenomena that are considered independent of individuals and, thus, collects numbers or data that can be quantified. Since qualitative research focuses on how individuals interpret their world (Snape and Spencer, 2003), it has to ask individuals to narrate their thoughts and experiences or observe individuals so as to understand how they behave in their natural environment. On this basis, qualitative research does not collect data that is quantifiable but instead focuses on words (Bryman, 2006).

The ways or methods of collecting data in quantitative and qualitative research rely on their ontological and epistemological grounds and differ accordingly. Quantitative research collects data through closed questionnaires and experiments and aims to collect data from a representative sample. A representative sample is important in quantitative research, because quantitative research aims to discover existing realities that apply to all individuals. Therefore, a large and representative sample means that the results can be generalised to the population. Quantitative researchers have to check the statistical power of their sample, and sampling is determined before data collection. Qualitative research uses methods that can provide detailed information in order to understand how individuals interpret their environment or phenomena. As a result, qualitative research uses methods such as in-depth interviews, focus groups, observation, analysis of texts, diaries and so forth. Though qualitative research can use representative samples, it largely aims to understand phenomena, behaviours or concepts in depth; hence, it is interested in the "conceptual power" of the sample (Onwuegbuzie and Collins, 2007: 283). Sampling in qualitative research cannot be determined before data collection, because researchers do not know how much their participants will express. Thus, sampling size is determined after data collection and is done through data or themes saturation. Data saturation refers to the point when a qualitative dataset stops offering new information or themes.

Interestingly, both quantitative and qualitative research methodologies have different quality markers. There are four main quality markers in quantitative research: (1) internal validity, (2) external validity, (3) reliability and (4) objectivity. Internal validity means that the study measures what it claims it measures, while external validity reflects the degree to which the results can be generalised. Reliability indicates that the study produces similar results over time, and objectivity means that no biases have influenced the collection of data and the results (Shenton, 2004). If these quality markers are met, this means that the study has achieved its goals in accordance with its theoretical grounds of realism and positivism; that is, it has discovered the external reality it aimed to discover. According to Guba (1981: 84–87), qualitative research has four equivalent quality markers: (1) credibility, (2) transferability, (3) dependability and (4) confirmability. Credibility is equivalent to internal validity and addresses the question of whether the study reflects reality. Transferability reflects generalisability in the sense that the results of one study could be transferred to the results of another study. Dependability is comparable to reliability in that qualitative researchers describe in detail their methodology, collection of data, coding and analysis in order for the study to be repeated by other researchers. Confirmability addresses objectivity, as the results reflect participants' understanding of reality and not that of the researcher. There is a fifth quality marker for qualitative research, which is the underlying force of the four markers outlined above. This is data or themes saturation. In order for qualitative researchers to meet the quality markers, they have to have enough data, and saturation is a marker for the appropriate amount of data before they can move on to the analysis (Constantinou *et al.*, 2017). Guest *et al.* (2006) termed saturation the "gold standard" in qualitative health science research (see also Morse, 2015; 1995).

The various theoretical grounds and practical pathways of research are outlined in Table 0.1. However, showing the different theoretical and practical pathways between quantitative and qualitative research does not mean that these two regimes of investigating social reality are mutually exclusive. Though quantitative researchers have argued that qualitative research is unscientific, and qualitative researchers have maintained that quantitative research is reductionist and can be authoritarian, the proponents of these two research methodologies have revisited their stance, amended their direction, and, many times, relied on both quantitative and qualitative findings to reach their conclusions (Phellas, 2012). On the one hand, though positivism is the dominant basis of quantitative research, quantitative research has now increasingly moved towards post-positivism. That is, quantitative researchers have acknowledged that reality can be culturally contingent, might be complex and should be subject to ethical regulations (O'Reilly and Kiyimba, 2015). Crotty (1998) indicated that even physicists have accepted the relativity of physical laws. On the other hand, qualitative researchers have shown that some qualitative studies can elicit generalisable results, and have found markers that can verify the quality of qualitative research (Shanton, 2004). Very often, studies use mixed methods in order to understand a phenomenon more holistically and in greater depth or when they aim to triangulate research findings (Pope *et al.*, 2007; Bryman, 2006). Despite the ontological, epistemological and methodological differences between quantitative and qualitative research, both aim to achieve the highest quality research possible, relying on specific research questions and adopting robust methodological procedures in order to produce usable results.

This book, entitled *Social Research in Health and Illness: Case-based Approaches*, presents both quantitative and qualitative research methodologies against the background of their contribution to understanding health and illness. For example, social scientists nowadays systematically investigate (1) the prevalence of diseases, (2) adherence to therapy, (3) patients' quality of life, (4) health services and health systems, (5) inequalities in health, (6) lay health beliefs, (7) experiences of chronic illness, (8) stigmatisation, (9) doctor–patient relationships, and so forth. This timely book aims to contribute to the increased demands of

Table 0.1 Research theoretical and practical pathways

Ontology	*Realism*	*Idealism*
Epistemological procedures	Deduction	Induction
Theory	Positivism	Interpretivism
Type of research	Quantitative research	Qualitative research
Research methods and data	Closed questionnaires, experiments, numerical data	Interviews, focus groups, observation, words and narratives
Quality markers	Internal validity, external validity, reliability, objectivity	Credibility, transferability, dependability, confirmability, saturation

researching health and illness, and focuses largely on chronic illness because of its prevalence in contemporary times.

The book was inspired by our rich experiences as both researchers and supervisors of postgraduate research. We noticed that researchers or early-stage researchers tended to underestimate the amount of work that high-quality research studies require. Many of them wanted to start collecting data before reading the literature on their topic or before fully understanding their research methodology. They also tended to underestimate the amount of information they needed for their qualitative research, omitting data saturation or the importance of their sample power in their quantitative studies. Furthermore, we identified that they lacked flexibility at the initial stages of their research and soon reached a dead end, which was often discouraging. Some researchers even dropped out at the very early stages of their research. Therefore, the idea for this book was conceived largely in order to fill in the procedural gaps in the research process and to highlight some important steps that need to be taken.

More specifically, the following five particular characteristics of the book make it stand out from other books on social research methods in health. First, the book presents social research in health in a friendly and accessible way by placing brainstorming questions throughout each chapter. Second, it applies the main principles of research to realistic, real-life cases which show (1) the dilemmas researchers may face at the beginning of their research journey, (2) the steps they have to take in order to properly explore their research questions, and (3) the choices they may have regarding the appropriate research methodology to address their research questions. Third, each chapter works as a brief review of the literature in the social aspects of the health condition it aims to explore. Fourth, it highlights the importance of reviewing the basic literature before finalising any research methodology procedures. Fifth, it introduces new methodological material, such as ways of achieving data saturation in qualitative research and of using the Internet as a research setting. The book is more suitable for postgraduate students and early-career researchers. This is because some background in social research methodology is required for the reader to obtain full benefit from the book. Also, it could be helpful for experienced researchers who want to use methodologies they have not used before. Both authors contributed to the write-up of the book. However, each author focused more on different chapters. That is, Professor Constantinos N. Phellas worked more closely on Chapters 2, 6, 7, 8 and 9, whereas Dr Costas S. Constantinou focused on Chapters 1, 3, 4, 5 and 10. Let us now introduce each chapter.

Chapter 1 focuses on how a systematic literature review should be carried out and presents three examples of systematic reviews. It describes the case of Annie Hirschfeld, who is an early-stage researcher and wishes to review the literature on the experience of chronic illness. She soon realises that her research question is too broad and that it has already been explored by other social scientists. As a result, she decides to refine her research question and learns more about the steps that should be followed in order to conduct an effective systematic literature review.

Chapter 2 aims to study diabetes I and II. Brian Bowie is interested in understanding the social experiences of patients living with Type I and Type II diabetes. Brian wants to compare the two types of diabetes to see whether they have a different impact on the lives of patients. Brian narrows down his research question to the investigation of patients' adherence to the therapy of diabetes I and II, and chooses the social survey as the most appropriate research methodology in order to adequately address his research question.

Chapter 3 describes the in-depth interview as a qualitative research method. In this chapter, Andrew Stefanides is a doctor who cannot understand from the findings of a quantitative research study why patients living with thalassaemia experience a worse quality of life than the healthy population. Andrew delves into the relevant literature in order to understand more about the social aspects of thalassaemia and states his research question as specifically as possible. He then reads the principles of qualitative research and in-depth interviews and pays particular attention to his sampling, as he wants to produce detailed and reliable results. He makes sure that he achieves data saturation on the basis of a specific methodology.

Chapter 4 presents the uses and usefulness of focus groups. Julie Anderson tries to interview patients living with multiple sclerosis, but finds that they were not telling her the whole truth regarding their experiences with the illness. Therefore, she considers forming patient focus groups in order to discuss their experiences. Julie is pleased to notice that the focus groups work better in this case. Like Andrew, Julie pays particular attention to achieving saturation of her data in order to make sure that she has sufficient data to proceed with analysis.

Another popular qualitative method is presented in Chapter 5. Alice Erickson uses the method of observation to understand how patients living with end-stage kidney disease experience haemodialysis. Alice initially uses a mixed method with closed questionnaires and interviews. However, she realises that there is more to what her patients tell her during interviews, and so she decides to conduct field observation to record the experience of haemodialysis in a natural setting: the haemodialysis room in a hospital. To conduct her research successfully, Alice learns more about how she can be an effective observer and how to saturate her data before she stops sampling.

Chapter 6 presents the case of John Bennett, a nurse, who believes that the residents of a large, outer-city community where he lives are more vulnerable to heart diseases than people residing elsewhere. He argues that the number of residents who die from heart problems in this area has escalated over the last few years. John is interested in conducting a study to test his hypothesis and decides that a longitudinal method is the best in this case. John will study a large number of people from a specific age cohort over a period of 10 years in order to understand the impact of various social factors on the incidence of heart disease.

In Chapter 7, Frank Stevenson, a researcher, is interested in studying people who live with HIV/AIDS in London. While there are quite a few quantitative and qualitative studies on patients living with HIV/AIDS, Frank wants to focus on married men and explore the changes in their lives and any incidents of stigmatisation they might have experienced. Interestingly, though he identifies potential participants, he finds that it is difficult to persuade them to participate. Patients are afraid of public exposure even though Frank assures them of confidentiality. Frank then considers the Internet as a research setting that might be better received by his potential participants.

Chapter 8 presents another quantitative methodology, that of secondary data analysis. Janet Gordon is a psychiatrist and is faced with a challenge from a psychiatric patient's relative who believes that mental hospitals are like prisons, whose aim is to prevent patients from socially interacting with the rest of society. The patient's relative also argues that the mental hospital where Janet is practising has always been a prison-like place for the mentally ill. Janet is interested in examining the hospital's archives in order to understand how the procedures of managing the patients have changed over the years.

After presenting various quantitative and qualitative research methods, Chapter 9 unfolds the case of James White, a doctor who treats older patients living with Alzheimer's disease and is interested in recording the number of changes in his patients' lives, as well as understanding what it means to live with Alzheimer's. James thinks that a combination of quantitative and qualitative research methods will provide him with a more holistic picture of his patients' experiences.

Chapter 10 aims to highlight the importance of ethics when conducting research. Mary Hanson is about to begin her research study on women living with breast cancer, focusing on both their quality of lives as well as their experience of the disease. Mary has obtained approval from institutional and national ethics committees, but she is slightly embarrassed when one of her participants asks the following questions after reading the informed consent form: "Will you record the interviews or will you take notes? How long will you keep your data? Will somebody else read my interview?" These are important ethical questions that Mary must address before commencing her research.

References

Bowling A (2014) *Research Methods in Health: Investigating Health and Health Services* (4th ed.). London: McGraw-Hill.

Bryman A (2006) Integrating quantitative and qualitative research: How is it done? *Qualitative Research* 6(1): 97–113.

Constantinou CS, Georgiou M and Pedikogianni M (2017) A comparative method for themes saturation (CoMeTS) in qualitative interviews. *Qualitative Research*. Epub ahead of print. DOI:10.1177/1468794116686650.

Guba EG (1981) Criteria for assessing the trustworthiness of naturalistic inquiries. *Education Communication and Technology* 29(2): 75–91.

Guest G, Bunce A and Johnson L (2006) How many interviews are enough? An experiment with data saturation and variability. *Field Methods* 18(1): 59–82.

Morse J (1995) The significance of saturation. *Qualitative Health Research* 5(2): 147–149.

Morse J (2015) "Data were saturated…" *Qualitative Health Research* 25(5): 587–588.

Onwuegbuzie AJ and Collins KMT (2007a) A typology of mixed methods sampling designs in social science research. *The Qualitative Report* 12(2): 281–316.

O'Reilly M and Kiyimba N (2015) *Advanced Qualitative Research: A Guide to Using Theory*. London: SAGE.

Ormston R, Spencer L, Barnard M and Snape D (2014) The foundations of qualitative research. In: Ritchie J, Lewis J, Nicholls CM and Ormston R (eds) *Qualitative Research Practice: A Guide for Social Science Students and Researchers*. London: SAGE, pp. 1–26.

Phellas C (2012) *Researching Non-Heterosexual Sexualities*. London: Ashgate.

Pope C, Mays N, and Popay J (2007) *Synthesizing Qualitative and Quantitative Health Evidence: A Guide to Methods*. Maidenhead: Open University Press.

Ryan AB (2006) Post-positivist approaches to research. In: *Researching and Writing your Thesis: A Guide for Postgraduate Students*. MACE: Maynooth Adult and Community Education, pp. 12–26.

Shenton AK (2004) Strategies for ensuring trustworthiness in qualitative research projects. *Education for Information* 22: 63–75.

Snape D and Spencer L (2003) The foundations of qualitative research. In Ritchie J and Lewis J (eds) *Qualitative Research Practice: A Guide for Social Science Students and Researchers*. London: SAGE, pp. 1–23.

1 Literature review

Experiencing chronic illness

Abstract

Annie Hirschfeld is an early-stage social researcher who has recently developed an interest in the field of health. Specifically, she wants to focus on chronic illness; however, before formulating any research proposals, she would like to explore the existing literature on how chronic illness has been studied as a social experience.

This chapter serves as an introduction to the following chapters on two levels. First, a review of the literature is necessary for all publications and research studies, regardless of the research method used. Therefore, this chapter is an introduction to how a literature review should be conducted pertaining to any studies and publications in the field of social sciences of health. Second, the chapter will also function as an introduction to the sociology of chronic illness preparing the grounds for understanding the research methods in more depth, which will be applied to specific chronic conditions in Chapters 2 to 10.

Learning objectives:

- Define what a literature review is.
- Explain the importance of reviewing the literature.
- Describe the steps involved in conducting a literature review.
- Outline the method of finding and examining the literature, as well as the process of presenting and discussing the results.

Scenario

Annie Hersfield is an early-stage social researcher who has recently developed an interest in the field of health. Specifically, she wants to focus on chronic illness; however, before formulating any research proposals, she would like to explore the existing literature on how chronic illness has been studied as a social experience. She begins by searching for information related to chronic illness. She first attempts this using the search engine Google Scholar and ends up with nearly three million references on the topic. Similar search engines, such as OVID, do not yield a different outcome. Annie is puzzled and worried; she cannot figure out whether she is doing something wrong. She decides to see whether she can identify any guidelines on how to conduct a literature review. She is relieved to find out that she was indeed doing something wrong and that she should have decided on a more focused and structured approach. What follows in the chapter is an amalgamation of information from Aveyard's (2010) *Literature Review in Health and Social Care: A Practical Guide*; Jesson and Lacey's (2006) *How to Do (or Not to Do) a Critical Literature Review*; *The Cochrane Collaboration Guide to Systematic Review*; basic textbooks in the field, such as Bowling's (2014) *Research Methods in Health: Investigating Health and Health Services* and Green and Thorogood's (2009) *Qualitative Methods for Health Research* as well as the authors' experiences. This is because all these sources share many similarities, and we thought to write a more general text that has been influenced by all of them. Wherever we draw on specific terms or procedures, we indicate the source more specifically.

Discuss

- What was Annie doing wrong?
- How can Annie be more organised and focused in her search?

Defining literature review

Annie wants to answer the question "How do patients experience chronic illness?" She aims to read as many resources as possible and summarise her findings in an analytical way. Given the difficulty she has already faced, it would be a good idea for her to revisit the relevant guides to better understand what a literature review is and how it could be carried out in an effective and scientific way.

Let us start with what a literature review is not. A literature review is not a series of summaries or a list of pieces of information found in existing published works. If a literature review consisted of summaries, it would be easily produced by stringing together a number of abstracts. Indeed, researchers often make the mistake of merely reading the abstract and not the entire resource. Given this, reviewing the literature entails more than simply summarising and, therefore, requires careful attention and dedication in order to produce a useful outcome.

According to Jesson and Lacey (2006: 140), a review of the literature is "a narrative account of information that is already currently available, accessible and published, which may be written from a number of differing paradigms or perspectives, depending on the standpoint of the writer". A "narrative account" refers to a text that is the reviewer's construct and links together the findings from the reviewed resources. Along similar lines, Aveyard (2010: 5) wrote: "a literature review is the comprehensive study and interpretation of literature that relates to a particular topic." To interpret and narrate their account effectively, researchers need to have a research question in mind when reviewing the relevant literature. In other words, a literature review is a methodology of researching and reviewing existing material and generating conclusions that do not exist in the individual resources reviewed. Thus, the resources selected for review are actually research data, which need to be well selected and directly relevant to the research question. The results need to be presented and discussed as in any other research study. So, Annie is expected to conduct a research study of existing resources and construct her narrative so as to present the results and the conclusions that she arrived at.

Discuss

- Why does Annie need to conduct a literature review? Why is it useful?
- Could Annie make any contribution to academic scholarship by reviewing the literature?

Why should researchers review the literature?

Now that we have explained what a literature review is, there are a few main reasons why Annie should review the literature. First, she needs to lay the ground for her own research; more specifically, Annie should be aware of what is already known about the area she is interested in researching and how much has already been answered in regard to her research question. Second, Annie should avoid duplicating research studies. Therefore, a thorough review of the literature would help her to make sure that what she wants to study has not yet been explored by other researchers. In this way, her research question is now justified, in the sense that she can demonstrate why there is a need to research what she wants to examine. In other words, instead of repeating studies already undertaken and published, reviewing the literature would help inform Annie of what research is missing in a particular area. Having to identify gaps in research and justify the need for researching particular topics or answering research questions is fundamental not only to the advancement of scholarship but also for securing external funds.

A third reason to conduct a literature review is in order to answer a specific research question by reviewing all the studies that have already been published. This does not entail having Annie write a series of summaries; rather, she would review the studies critically and reach a conclusion that is not found in any of the individual studies. In other words, Annie's conclusion would go beyond what one would read in the individual studies. This requires a deep understanding of the studies or resources used and a well-developed academic imagination in order to put forward new conclusions based on the previous ones. So, Annie may discover new terrain that had not been identified in the individual resources reviewed, or she may identify gaps in the literature, which need to be addressed through further research. Finally, through the review of the literature, Annie has the opportunity to critically evaluate research methodologies. She may find that the methodologies used so far to study a phenomenon have not been adequate and may suggest the use of different methodologies or a combination.

What types of literature review are there?

Literature reviews can take three main forms, which reflect the reviewers' intentions and plans. First, a literature review can be done chronologically. In choosing to do so, researchers would need to locate all the relevant articles, place them in chronological order and present the findings from the articles according to time periods. In the social sciences, chronological reviews would be very helpful in the case of exploring what has been written, for example, about specific concepts, or to check whether the quality of life and experiences of patients change over time. Alternatively, a literature review could be conducted thematically. A thematic literature review refers to a review that focuses on a specific theme or phenomenon and explores what has been published about it. This is the most common type of literature review and provides researchers with substantial evidence about what is already known and how further research could be developed. The third type of literature review is that which focuses on the research methodologies employed. Here, researchers do not focus on the content but on the methodologies used in order to come up with conclusions about weaknesses in the methodologies and/or results and future prospects.

Interestingly, a literature review is not always confined to one form; it may combine the different types of review. For example, Pierret's (2003) review (described further later in this chapter) is a combination of chronological and thematic, while other reviews may explore both the content and research methodologies. Based on these three main types, Annie decides to conduct a thematic review of the literature. Her theme is the experience of chronic illness, but an initial literature search indicated that her topic may be too broad. She now needs to think of ways to narrow it down and to have a clear plan of how she will effectively perform the review.

Based on a theoretical approach, Annie could do a meta-analysis, a meta-ethnography or a meta-study. Aveyard (2010) explained that a meta-analysis involves the combination of quantitative studies in order to find a statistical result, which may not be very obvious in the individual studies. A meta-ethnography refers to the combination of results from qualitative studies. Other scholars have named this a meta-synthesis (Sim and Madden, 2008). In meta-ethnographies, reviewers combine results from qualitative studies and also discuss the methodologies and theories employed. Annie chooses to carry out a meta-ethnography and to combine results from various qualitative studies, since she is focusing on how patients experience illness, which has been explored rigorously by qualitative research.

How should a literature review be carried out?

The question may seem simple to answer, but, in reality, carrying out a literature review is a challenging endeavour. Many people think that a literature review is a summary of a number of articles on a particular topic. However, a literature review is more complicated than that, as researchers should adopt a systematic approach and have a review schedule starting from the question they are examining and continuing on to searching for data, selecting resources based on well-defined inclusion and exclusion criteria, exhausting the literature, reading, summarising, critically appraising and, finally, discussing the way forward. The Cochrane Collaboration (2006) prepared a detailed guide as to how a systematic review should be carried out. The guide places emphasis on having at least two people performing the literature review independently in order to ensure quality and to minimise errors.

Let us explain the process of deciding on a specific research question before starting to search through the databases. Annie has to decide on a specific research question; otherwise, she may find herself in an endless process of reading and reviewing resources. In other words, the research question functions like a compass or a framework within which Annie can work. The research question, therefore, should be neither too broad nor too narrow. If it is very broad, Annie will not manage to have a focused review and may end up spending much more time than expected or scheduled. On the other hand, if the research question is too narrow, Annie may undertake a superficial review due to the scarcity of relevant resources.

Therefore, what is a good way to finalise a research question? Annie could take note of specific areas that derive from her general observations. These self-observed topics can work as guides at the beginning. Then, she can explore the literature to identify any similar topics that have been researched. By reading the relevant literature on similar topics, she can refine her research question and focus only on the most relevant resources. Though Annie initially had in mind a broad idea to explore (i.e. illness experience), she now thinks to focus on a specific condition and investigate how patients experience it. More specifically, she wants to focus on end-stage kidney disease and patients' experiences of haemodialysis. However, she aims to end up with a topic that is neither too broad nor too narrow. For example, Annie may observe that older dialysis patients express more positive attitudes towards dialysis itself compared with their younger counterparts. This question is a bit narrow, because it focuses not only on a specific disease treatment but also on age groups and the way they express themselves towards medical technology. Reading the literature, she may realise that there are not enough studies to review and discuss relating to such an observation. Annie, however, may decide to make her topic a bit broader by answering the question of how patients with end-stage kidney disease experience haemodialysis. On these grounds, Annie could refine her research question to "What is the impact of haemodialysis on patients' social life and identity?" (This topic is further analysed in Chapter 5, which discusses the main research findings in the social aspects of haemodialysis and how observation can help researchers understand patients in their natural environment.) Annie will explore what has been published on her research question and critically appraise the articles reviewed.

Having refined her research question, Annie now needs to select all the resources that are relevant to this specific question. However, how could Annie decide precisely what is relevant and what is not? Annie could have clearly defined inclusion and exclusion criteria in order to make sure that she only reviews the resources that are relevant to her research question. Annie then decides to set the following inclusion criteria. First, research studies should have been published in academic journals; second, articles should have been published during the last 10 years; and third, the research studies should focus on how haemodialysis has influenced patients' social lives, family lives, employment and workplace, leisure activities, peers and the sense of self. Put differently, Annie is looking for studies that have explored how haemodialysis has influenced patients as social beings. Thus, Annie will exclude studies of peritoneal dialysis, patients' cognitive and emotional processes, books, book reviews, reports and perspectives.

Discuss

- Now that she has finalised her research question, what should Annie's next steps be?

With a clear research question in mind, Annie now needs to start searching databases in order to identify potential articles for her review. There are many databases that Annie could search for articles, such as PubMed, OVID, Medline, PsycINFO, Sociological Abstracts and so forth. The databases used should relate to the general area of interest – social sciences and health. As Annie is focusing on the social aspects of haemodialysis, she could also explore more specialised journals, such as *Social Science & Medicine*, *Journal of Health and Social Behaviour*, *Sociology of Health & Illness*, *Qualitative Health Research* and *Health*, which are the main sociological journals that publish studies on health, illness and medicine.

Interestingly, Annie wonders how she should search. She could make a short list of topics based on her experiences so far and a few resources on how patients experience chronic illness. For instance, these topics could be *identity*, *family relations*, *stigma*, *discrimination*, *biography* and *disruption*, and could serve as keywords, which Annie would use when searching through databases or specialised journals. Annie may also combine these keywords with *haemodialysis* or *end-stage kidney/renal disease/failure* in order to focus the articles as closely as possible to her research question. When Annie finds all the potential research articles, she should then proceed with an initial screening by carefully reading both the titles and the abstracts in order to make the final selection based on her inclusion and exclusion criteria. Whenever she is not sure, she should read the whole article to decide whether it should be selected for her review or not.

When Annie has exhausted her search based on her inclusion and exclusion criteria, she then has to read thoroughly all the articles that will make up her review. She must read and review each article individually before she synthesises, discusses and concludes. Reading requires organisation, and Annie decides to read, summarise and critically appraise each article. Summarising should be as extensive as possible so that Annie can have information about the methodology, research findings and general conclusions from each article. To critically appraise, Annie will need to discuss the weaknesses and strengths of the article, in particular the research methodology, as well as the analysis and interpretation of the results. More specifically, Aveyard (2010: 111–116) suggested a number of questions to be used as tools for critically appraising articles. These are: Who wrote the paper? Where is the paper published? Is there a research question and is the method appropriate for addressing the question? Was the right qualitative research method used? What was the sample for the study? How big was the sample? How were the data collected? How were the data analysed?

Having detailed summaries for each article will help Annie to synthesise, discuss and go beyond what is found in the individual articles. However, what does synthesising actually mean? Annie could initially include the articles that meet her inclusion criteria in a table and organise the information into categories: authors, date, methodology and important summary points. Through synthesising, Annie could then code and group articles together on the basis of narrower sections, such as family relations, employment, leisure time and so forth, reflecting the key words she used to identify the articles. Under each section, Annie can construct her own academic narrative, which embeds extended information from the articles she has summarised. It is a narrative because it is her own construction, but it is of academic nature in the sense that it represents the articles she reviewed. This synthesis resembles the process of analysing qualitative data (see Chapters 3 and 4).

To explain further, Annie should start her review of each section by writing a few sentences that would work as a collective description of all relevant articles in that section. Then, she should write, in more detail, the relevant findings from each article as a way to support her collective description. Annie should carry on organising her section into sub-sections and follow the same procedure until she cannot identify any other collective descriptions. Annie should also be mindful of the "hierarchy of evidence" (Aveyard, 2010: 137) and present the most important evidence first under each section. This will help Annie to structure her material. Furthermore, under each section or sub-section, Annie should critically appraise the articles by discussing each study's weaknesses and strengths as well as why studies of similar research questions produce different findings. Possible reasons could include the use of different theoretical approaches and methodologies, socio-historical influences and so forth. After synthesising information from the selected articles, in the discussion part of her literature review, Annie could use her academic imagination to come up with arguments that cannot be found in the selected articles. These arguments could lead to a general conclusion about the impact of haemodialysis on a patient's social life, gaps in the literature and suggestions for future research.

Examples of literature reviews

Annie reads examples of how other researchers have reviewed the literature in areas that are relevant to illness experience in order to better understand how the guidelines she read above can be applied. She starts with a more generic review of the literature by Pierret (2003), who focused on the illness experience, and then continues with more focused reviews such as "transition" (Kralik *et al.*, 2006) and the experience of fibromyalgia syndrome (Sim and Madden, 2008).

Chronic illness experience

Pierret (2003) published a critical review of the literature entitled "The illness experience: state of knowledge and perspectives for research". Pierret aimed to review relevant articles published by the journal *Sociology of Health & Illness*, but she was concerned about the likelihood of leaving out an important article. To ensure that this would not happen, Pierret set three inclusion criteria. First, the articles should directly address the perspective of those who experience a disease. Second, the articles should explore chronic illness in the sense that the illness becomes part of patients' identity over time. Third, the articles should investigate the consequences of illness and how these consequences are experienced by patients and the people around them. The use of inclusion criteria helped Pierret to select all the relevant articles and, at the same time, narrow her focus and, consequently, make it more manageable. Based on these criteria, Pierret reviewed 47 articles and two review essays. Pierret organised her literature review in themes based on the content of articles she reviewed. That is, she started with the "emergence of the illness experience in research" and carried on with "the subjectivity of the illness experience", "strategies of coping" and the "research experience of social structure". She ended with a section on future direction of research based on the gaps she identified from the existing research. Let us now go through Pierret's sections in more detail.

Under the "emergence of the illness experience in research" theme, Pierret discussed the emergence of studies related to this area in the 1960s and 1970s, when research focused primarily on Parson's concept of the sick role; a decade later, studies added the importance of various factors in how illness was experienced, such as stress and coping. These initial studies were not published in *Sociology of Health & Illness*, because the journal was established in 1979. The creation of this journal contributed significantly to the evolution of research and theory in the area of illness experience. A highly influential article was published by Michael Bury in 1982 and analysed the concept of "biographical disruption" based on empirical evidence. Through 30 semi-structured interviews with people with rheumatoid arthritis, Bury explained that biographical disruption referred to the upsetting of patients' normal life and identity and had three dimensions: the disruption of the patient's daily routine, the patient's biography and identity, and how the patient responded to such disruption.

Pierret then carried on reviewing articles that addressed the issue of "the subjectivity of illness experience". She explained that patients initially searched for meaning, trying to understand what had happened and why, and positioning themselves and the disease in the world. Apart from the quest for meaning, patients experience stigma. Pierret presented Scambler and Hopkins' (1986) concepts of "enacted" and "felt" stigma. The first refers to being discriminated against because of a condition, whereas the second has to do with feeling ashamed or devalued due to having a disease or impairment. Pierret further discussed the subjectivity of illness experience by reviewing articles that explored the influence of social variables (e.g. age) on how patients experienced health conditions. For example, Pound *et al.* (1998) found that older patients considered suffering a stroke to be normal and expected. An important dimension of the illness experience is not only how patients experience their condition but also how they narrate it; that is, how they communicate it to other people and researchers. Illness narratives are reconstructions of a patient's experience that patients themselves make in order to make sense of their new self and to communicate this new self to others.

An interesting question addressed by Pierret was the strategies patients employed in order to cope with illness consequences. Here, Pierret focused on coping with stigma, the ways patients reorganised their life in order to accommodate the needs derived from their health condition, participation in patient groups, the use and importance of religion, and the usefulness of technology for both ameliorating illness consequences and dealing with stigma. The last topic that Pierret discussed was the impact of social structure on illness experience. Pierret found articles that discussed the impact of health policies, healthcare systems, medical knowledge and the mass media on how people experience their disease. For example, a new development in medical knowledge in regard to HIV improved patients' quality of life and, thus, the way they understood and experienced their condition. In this last section, Pierret formulated a discussion and suggested that more robust research should focus on the relationship between subjectivity and social structure.

Annie can see that her initial idea, to carry out a literature review of illness experience, has already been undertaken and published. Therefore, it would be preferable for her to change her research focus. Furthermore, though she found that her first topic was too broad, Pierret managed to review the literature effectively because she focused on the articles published by *Sociology of Health & Illness* only and thus kept her pool of articles restricted and manageable.

Transition in chronic illness

Transition is a term used in the social sciences of illness experience and pertains to the transitional state patients find themselves in when they are between being healthy and ill. In their paper entitled "Transition: A literature review" published in the *Journal of Advanced Nursing*, Kralik *et al.* (2006) reviewed a number of studies and presented a critical account of the ways the term "transition" has been used. The authors presented the definition of transition, which they had come up with in an earlier study, as "a process of convoluted passage during which people redefine their sense of self and develop self-agency in response to disruptive live events" (van Loon and Karlik, 2005; cited in Kralik *et al.* 2006: 321). The authors argued that understanding more about the transition of patients could assist in better comprehending how patients perceive their condition and their future and could improve communication with patients and treatment. Therefore, they did not have a very narrow research question, but aimed instead at reviewing the work that was published on the concept. They found many articles through the databases Medline, CINAHL, Sociofile and Psychlit. To ensure a manageable number of resources, they set the following inclusion criteria: research articles published between 1994 and 2004, articles that use transition as a main concept, and articles relevant to health and social behaviour. To make sure that they would locate all relevant articles, the authors drew from a number of relevant articles the following key words: social, life events, illness, crisis, identity and self. From this search, 45 potential articles were located. The authors screened all the articles through the inclusion criteria and decided to exclude 22 of them.

In reviewing the remaining 23 articles, Kralik *et al.* found that studies of chronic illness use the term "transition" to make reference to a change or move from one state to another. The literature does not show this change to be static but rather, a process of transformation. Kralik *et al.* outlined Van Gennep's theory of the "rites of passage" to indicate that transition may be a long process and it is staged. Transition is experienced when people's routine life is disrupted and there is no immediate way back to normality. Therefore, individuals need to go through a process of transformation themselves. The majority of articles reviewed showed that they used transition to explain what patients with chronic illness went through when they learned about their condition, while some articles referred to transition after the development of a condition, such as haemodialysis. What is strongly affected during the transition from being healthy to being ill is self-identity. This could take two directions: either the patient transforms in a negative way or the patient finds new meaning to life and undertakes new tasks. Kralik *et al.* concluded that understanding transition in chronic illness has implications within the nursing professions, since nurses can now better comprehend the transformation patients go through and thus contribute to a smooth transition to a patient's new state of self and routine.

Kralik *et al.*'s review was purely thematic and was narrow enough to explore how published studies have used the term "transition". Though Annie initially wanted to do a thematic review of this kind, she later realised that she wanted to do a thematic review around a specific condition, end-stage kidney disease and haemodialysis, which is on a par with the next example of a literature review.

Fibromyalgia syndrome (FMS)

Sim and Madden (2008) reviewed the literature with regard to the experience of fibromyalgia syndrome (FMS). Their review was entitled "Illness experience in fibromyalgia syndrome: A metasynthesis of qualitative studies" published in *Social Science & Medicine*. The authors started their review with an introduction to FMS and explained that it is diagnosed based on "chronic widespread pain, sleep disturbance, fatigue, and bilateral tender points" (Raspe and Croft, 1995: 57). One of the areas explored by a number of scholars is how people with FMS experience the syndrome. Therefore, the authors proceeded with a synthesis of qualitative studies aiming to understand the impact of FMS on patients and how patients understood it. The authors clarified that the purpose of their review was not to present summaries of a number of qualitative studies but to go beyond these summaries and come up with an overall experience of FMS based on how patients from the individual studies experienced the syndrome. Following the standard structure of a scientific paper, Sim and Madden organised their remaining review into methods, results, discussion and conclusion.

The authors proceeded with an online search of databases such as Medline, CINAHL, Social Science Citation Index, Science Citation Index, Sociofile, PsycINFO, Sociological Abstracts and AMED. They used the following keywords: fibromyalgia, qualitative, interview, subjective and experience. Based on the results, they looked into both the abstracts and the references. Having screened all the articles based on the abstracts, Sim and Madden included only the studies that explored the subjective experience of patients with FMS and excluded all studies that used quantitative methodologies, though these studies focused on the psychosocial aspects of the syndrome. To determine which articles should be selected for the final review, the authors continued with a second, more thorough screening based on Popay *et al.*'s (1998) seven categories for checking suitability. For example, under the criterion "illumination of subjective meaning", there was the question "Does the research, as reported, illuminate the subjective meaning, actions, and context of those being researched?" Both authors collaborated in order to reach consensus on what should be the answer to this question. By doing so, consistency between the authors was achieved.

In the results section of their review, Sim and Madden explained that they initially located 280 reports but ended up with 41. These 41 reports went through further filtering based on well-defined criteria. This resulted in 23 studies, which presented findings related to 383 participants. The authors constructed a table that included information about the authors, data collection, data analysis and methodological limitations. Sim and Madden organised the results section into sub-sections in order to present what they found from the 23 studies about the subjective experience of FMS. They had findings under the following headings: experience of symptoms, searching for a diagnosis, legitimacy and coping. For the experience of symptoms, the authors explained that pain was the most common symptom. The location of pain varied, while some patients said that the pain was both physical and mental. Patients found it difficult to describe the pain and used metaphors instead, such as burning, boiling, cutting and so on. Fatigue was another symptom they experienced, while psychological problems were presented as a consequence of pain and fatigue. Searching for diagnosis was an important aspect of patients' experience, because they were anxious and worried about not having a diagnosis at all. Therefore, as the results showed, patients felt relieved when they had an official medical diagnosis, as they now hoped that they would be cured. Patients, interestingly, did not look only for an official diagnosis but also for legitimacy. Since their symptoms could not easily be identified and their physical appearance did not match their experiences, patients had difficulty explaining to other people what they really had, and other people had difficulty accepting that a health condition was present. Patients tried to cope with FMS. They needed, first, to clearly understand FMS and second, to find ways through social support groups and family to accept that FMS was a legitimate condition and learn how to better manage it.

In the discussion section of their review, Sim and Madden went beyond the findings described above. They used their academic imagination in order to come up with a grand experience of FMS, which would be representative of the studies reviewed. That is, patients experienced symptoms in certain ways, searched for a diagnosis and legitimacy, and tried to cope with FMS. However, these are not all separate and fixed experiences; rather, they are intertwined. More specifically, some patients relied on the biomedical model in order to describe their pain in an attempt to make it more acceptable and thus legitimate. However, other patients resorted to a Cartesian dualist approach to the body and mind, which results in confused feelings about FMS. Such ambiguity added to the sense of illegitimacy; when they felt that their condition was illegitimate, patients adopted specific coping strategies to compensate for this. For example, they hid their condition or participated in patient groups. Sim and Madden argued that patients who used the biomedical model to explain their disease and their experience resonated with the biomedical definition of FMS and appeared to be more successful in coping with the syndrome.

Conclusion

Annie learned that a literature review is a distinct research methodology and the selected studies to be reviewed are actually data for analysis and interpretation. Annie needed to formulate a clear and feasible research question, as she would do in any other research project. Then, she had to decide on a specific methodology for locating and screening the resources to review by putting down well-defined keywords and inclusion/exclusion criteria. Having found and selected the final resources to be included in the review, Annie needed to present the most important findings in sections and sub-sections. Then, Annie had to discuss and interpret the results. The discussion section is where Annie needed to activate her academic imagination and come up with additional results that would not be found in any of the individual resources but would represent them as a whole. In other words, these grand results would be "greater than the sum of the parts" (Campbell *et al.*, 2003: 672). By the end of this lesson, Annie felt more confident and comfortable in commencing her own review to answer the question "What is the impact of haemodialysis on people's social life and identity?" by reading the studies conducted by other researchers.

References

Aveyard H (2010) *Literature Review in Health and Social Care* (2nd ed.). Berkshire: Open University Press.

Bowling A (2014) *Research Methods in Health: Investigating Health and Health Services* (4th ed.). Berkshire: McGraw-Hill.

Bryman A (2001) *Social Research Methods*. Oxford: Oxford University Press.

Green J and Thorogood N (2009) *Qualitative Methods for Health Research* (2nd ed.). Los Angeles: SAGE.

Higgins JPT and Green S (eds) (2006) *The Cochrane Collaboration Handbook for Systematic Reviews in Interventions*. Chichester, UK: John Wiley & Sons.

Jesson J and Lacey F (2006) How to do (or not to do) a critical literature review. *Pharmacy Education* 6(2): 139–148.

Kralik D, Visentin K and Van Loon A (2006) Transition: A literature review. *Journal of Advanced Nursing* 55(3): 320–329.

Pierret J (2003) The illness experience: State of knowledge and perspectives for research. *Sociology of Health & Illness* 25: 4–22.

Schutt R (2004) *Investigating the Social World: The Process and Practice of Research* (4th ed.). Los Angeles: SAGE.

Sim J and Madden S (2008) Illness experience in fibromyalgia: A metasynthesis of qualitative studies. *Social Science & Medicine* 67: 57–67.

2 Social survey

Diabetes type I and type II

Abstract

Brian Bowie, a postgraduate student, is interested in understanding the social experiences of patients living with diabetes type I and II. Brian wants to compare the two types of diabetes to see whether they have a different impact on the lives of patients. Though the prevalence of diabetes is quite high, he is uncertain as to how to study as many patients as possible.

This chapter focuses on the social survey as a research tool that can be used to study large samples. The chapter begins by outlining the social aspects of diabetes, which can help Brian refine his research question, and moves on to discuss the processes involved in the design and implementation of a social survey.

Learning objectives:

- Present the sociological literature on the social aspects of diabetes type I and II.
- Describe the purpose, as well as the advantages and disadvantages, of conducting social surveys.

Scenario

Brian Bowie, a postgraduate student, is interested in understanding the social experiences of patients living with diabetes type I and II. Brian wants to compare the two types of diabetes to see whether they have a different impact on the lives of patients. Though the prevalence of diabetes is quite high, he is uncertain about how to study as many patients as possible. Conducting in-depth interviews might be an option; however, interviews would limit generalisations and comparison between the two types. In order to refine his research question and decide on a methodology, Brian decides to delve into the relevant literature.

Discuss

- How could the literature help Brian?
- How could the literature shed light on people with diabetes?
- What might be the most appropriate research methodology for Brian to use?
- Could information about people living with diabetes help Brian with his research question and research methodology? In which ways?

The psychosocial aspects of diabetes type I and II

According to the National Institute for Health and Care Excellence (NICE) Guideline on Diabetes Mellitus (2006), the prevalence of diabetes is higher in males (2.3 per cent) than in females (1.4 per cent). The international literature indicates that people with diabetes have to confront several psychological and behavioural changes throughout their life due to the disease, including alterations to their basic life habits (diet and exercise) (Sriram *et al.*, 2005). A multinational survey conducted by Nicolucci *et al.* (2013), aiming to evaluate the psychosocial outcomes in 8596 people with diabetes type I and II, found that diabetes had a negative impact on several aspects: for 20.5 per cent on their relationships with family and friends, and for 62.2 per cent on their physical health. Furthermore, diabetes medication was perceived as an obstacle to their ability to live a normal life.

In addition, a study conducted by Hapunda *et al.* (2015) in Zambia, aiming to explore the quality of healthcare and barriers to quality care of 12 adolescents living with diabetes type I as well as the perceptions of 12 stakeholders (8 caregivers and 4 health practitioners) on changes due to the disease that affected both patients and their families, found that adolescents experienced stigma due to the incorrect belief of their peers that diabetes was a communicable disease. Further, several adjustments to their lives have also been underlined, such as the inability to enjoy previous activities for fear of low blood sugar levels or due to their parents' overprotection. In relation to their quality of life, diabetes was perceived to be associated with a shorter life expectancy due to poor healthcare systems and socioeconomic circumstances as well as lifestyle choices.

A grounded theory study was conducted in Canada (Protudjer *et al.*, 2014) in order to explore the lived experiences of eight youngsters living with type II diabetes, as well as barriers and facilitators to adopting lifestyle approaches for diabetes self-management. The study concluded that barriers to the self-management of diabetes included participants' poor income as well as community violence and bullying. Regarding the lived experience of diabetes and the feelings relating to the first diagnosis, these included devastation, fear of disclosure due to prejudice, and feelings of denial. Further, Irani *et al.* (2014) conducted an action research study with 47 individuals with type I diabetes in Iran to identify strategies that would help them overcome the related stigma. Results showed that community-based strategies (e.g. education, advocacy contact and protest) could help people overcome the stigma related to diabetes. However, the effectiveness of the programme depends on the individual's involvement and the local conditions.

Sriram *et al.* (2005) conducted a study through questionnaires with a sample of 226 patients with diabetes (143 males and 83 females). The results highlight that females reported a higher score on anxiety, whereas males were found to be more satisfied with their life in general. Their stress level in relation to their disease was found to be lower than in females, and they reported that their health was improving. This was in line with other studies (Rubin *et al.*, 2006). Males were found to cope with diabetes better than females. However, their sex lives were reported to be impaired due to diabetes (Sriram *et al.*, 2005). Gender differences in people living with diabetes were also revealed through a review conducted by Jonsson *et al.* (2000), in which men were found to be more worried about the limitations that diabetes might impose on their lives (Jonsson *et al.*, 2000, cited in Gucciardi *et al.*, 2008). Other studies indicate that men believe that they can control their disease (Brown *et al.*, 2000, cited in Gucciardi *et al.*, 2008). Moreover, distinct levels of social support are also identified in the international literature among men and women (Nielsen *et al.*, 2006, cited in Gucciardi *et al.*, 2008). For example, men underlined the social support they received from their family in relation to nutritional management (Brown *et al.*, 2000, cited in Gucciardi *et al.*, 2008).

In the cross-sectional study of Adal *et al.* (2015), which aimed to explore the presence and extent of depressive symptoms following a diagnosis of type I diabetes mellitus in 295 adolescents in Turkey, no connection was found between gender and depression. A study conducted by Li *et al.* (2013), aiming to understand the lived experience as well as ways of coping adopted by 10 Chinese women with diabetes through semi-structured interviews, connected the physical symptoms of type II diabetes with feeling anxious and hopeless. It also noted women's decision not to disclose their health condition to their significant other for fear that this might negatively affect their relationship.

A qualitative study conducted in Canada (Mathew *et al.*, 2012) to explore the differences in self-management (specifically needs, barriers and challenges) among 17 men and 18 women living with type II diabetes mellitus revealed that women were more forthcoming about their diabetic identity, whereas men avoided social activities so as to protect themselves from exposing their specific dietary needs. Furthermore, distinct sources of social support were also mentioned by men and women. Men perceived their partner as a source of social support and noted that their families helped them adopt lifestyle changes and diet modifications (Mathew *et al.*, 2012).

Discuss

- What does the information from the literature tell Brian?
- How can this brief review of the relevant literature help Brian?
- What research method might be useful for Brian?

Brian still wants to study as many patients as possible, and he is excited to learn from the literature that different groups of patients (e.g. men and women) experience diabetes differently. Brian finds the relevant literature particularly helpful because it shows that diabetes has an impact on many aspects of the lives of patients. In order to study such impacts in a valid way, and to be able to compare between type I and type II diabetes as well as between various groups of patients based on demographic characteristics (gender, education age, employment etc.), Brian decides to narrow his research question; that is, to explore patients' adherence to therapy and its relationship with patients' quality of life.

To address this research question, Brian will use standardised and validated tools, which measure adherence and quality of life, and will include a section at the end of the questionnaire to record demographic data, which Brian can use to check for any correlations. Brian is still concerned about the number of patients to be included in his study. He considers using a social survey, but he is worried about how much time it will take to distribute the questionnaire and locate survey participants. He turns to the relevant literature for further insight before he finalises his decision.

Discuss

- What is a survey?
- Can a social survey help Brian address his research question?
- Could Brian consider other research methods for addressing his research question adequately?

What is a survey?

One of the best-known quantitative forms of methodology used in social and behavioural sciences is the survey. A survey is a field research approach that deals with the formulation of hypotheses and the testing of the relationship between non-manipulated variables (Kothari, 2004). There are different types of surveys: census surveys, ad hoc sample surveys, social surveys, economic surveys, public opinion surveys and Internet-based surveys.

Census surveys are surveys that represent the complete enumeration of all items in the population. Additionally, social surveys are social scientific endeavours used to explore attitudes, beliefs and behaviour, whereas economic surveys review the development of economic aspects through the comparison of the economy in the past, present and future (Kothari, 2004). Public opinion surveys refer to a specific sample and are designed to represent the opinions of a population through a series of questions. These are then generalised using ratios or confidence intervals (Kothari, 2004). Ad hoc sample surveys constitute a multi-purpose research design (and can be adopted by almost all social science disciplines and research topics).

In surveys, the application of sampling allows the production of descriptive statistics, representative (on a national, regional or state basis) of the whole study population, although at a much lower cost than with a census of every member of the population in question. To ensure that their study will produce statistically significant results, researchers make sure that they calculate the statistical power of their samples (Bowling, 2014) before they decide on the sample size. Sample surveys allow associations between factors to be mapped and measured (Hakim, 1987). Also, they can be used to study causal processes and to develop and test explanations for particular associations or social patterns. In developing countries, they are used for topics not covered by the population census in order to provide descriptive national or local statistics. Still, there are some limitations to using a sample survey, since it involves the use of a structured questionnaire, which obtains less depth and quality of information than an in-depth interview. Surveys can be used for studying individuals, social roles and social networks.

Additionally, some of the best-known designs to be used in a survey are cross-sectional, repeated cross-sectional, panel and mixed-method designs (Visser *et al.*, 2000). Cross-sectional surveys include data collection at a single point in time from a sample drawn from a particular population, often used to document the prevalence of particular characteristics in a population (e.g. the frequency with which people perform certain behaviours or the number of people who hold particular attitudes or beliefs), to assess relations between variables and differences between subgroups in a population or to test causal hypotheses (e.g. the use of a two-stage least squares regression in order to estimate the causal impact of variable A on variable B as well as the effect of variable B on variable A). A single cross-sectional survey can be used to assess the impact of a social event (e.g. priming in a real-world setting) (Visser *et al.*, 2000).

Repeated cross-sectional surveys involve data collection from independent samples drawn from the same population at two or more points in time. In addition, they can be used to investigate the impact of social events that occurred between the surveys (Weisberg *et al.*, 1995, cited in Visser *et al.*, 2000) and can be combined into a single dataset for statistical analysis, using information from one survey to estimate parameters in another survey (Brehm and Rahn, 1997, cited in Visser *et al.*, 2000).

Panel surveys involve data collection from the same people at two or more points in time and can be used to investigate the impact of social events (Visser *et al.*, 2000). Some disadvantages of panel surveys are as follows: the use of multiple interviews may result in a low response rate; the representativeness of the survey is threatened if some participants were interviewed at first and then do not agree to participate in subsequent waves of interviewing; participation in the initial survey may sensitise respondents to the issues under investigation, thus changing the phenomena being studied, and, as a result, respondents may give special attention or thought to these issues, which may alter their subsequent survey responses; and participants may want to stay consistent with answers given previously, thus masking genuine changes over time. To overcome all these disadvantages, researchers could combine cross-sectional and panel surveys into a single study (Visser *et al.*, 2000).

Experiments within surveys involve the random assignment of participants to "treatment" and "control" groups; differences between the two groups can then be attributed to the treatment. Each design described here can be altered to incorporate experimental manipulations. A random selection of participants can be exposed to one version of a questionnaire, while other respondents are exposed to another version. Differences in responses can then be attributed to the specific elements that were varied (Visser *et al.*, 2000). The advantages of using experiments within surveys are as follows: survey evidence documents that phenomena are widespread enough to be observable in the general population, in contrast to the generalisability issue of laboratory findings; estimates of effect size from surveys provide a more accurate basis for assessing the significance that any psychological process is likely to have in the course of daily life; and general population samples allow researchers to explore whether attributes of people that are homogeneous in the lab (but vary dramatically in the general population) moderate the effects or the processes producing them (Kinder and Sanders, 1990, cited in Visser *et al.*, 2000).

Steps involved in conducting a survey

First and foremost, the researcher should articulate the reasons for choosing and using a survey to explore the specific research questions, as well as clarifying the rationale behind conducting the survey in terms of purpose and in relation to existing theory and knowledge as well as in relation to the implications for practice (Yates, 2004). Hence, it is imperative to clarify as well as justify the reasons for choosing the survey as the most suitable methodology for his or her study. Furthermore, the researcher needs to allocate the roles of the research team (e.g. design development, data collection etc.) and to explain the expected outcomes of the survey (The Health Communication Unit at the Centre for Health Promotion, 1999). As with other research designs, a researcher should take the end users into consideration to avoid missing data, as well as specifying the population of interest for surveying (demographics, ways of communication, determining their similarities or differences to avoid sample heterogeneity, etc.), and determine the exact sample for the survey (The Health Communication Unit at the Centre for Health Promotion, 1999).

Next, the researcher should consider all the available resources in order to conduct the survey within the available budget. Undoubtedly, the researcher should assess the internal as well as external resources available. Internal resources that should be assessed refer to the budget allocated, the number of available researchers and their capacity to be involved with the research project, access to equipment and the development of a feasible timetable (The Health Communication Unit at the Centre for Health Promotion, 1999).

In relation to the capacity of the researchers to be involved, they must be capable of developing a questionnaire, deciding on the sampling design and the recruitment methods, using a word processor, being organised, communicating by phone, verifying data, coding as well as analysing data, and drafting research reports, as well as possessing presentation skills (The Health Communication Unit at the Centre for Health Promotion, 1999). It follows that the researcher needs to find the most suitable method to be used in relation to the project's aims and objectives as well as the disposable budget and the timetable during which the research will be completed (The Health Communication Unit at the Centre for Health Promotion, 1999).

Brian confirms that he will do a cross-sectional social survey. He now has a clear research question, which relates to patients' adherence to therapy and quality of life, and he wants to study as many patients as possible in order to have enough data for comparison between patients living with diabetes type I and type II with regard to their demographical characteristics, such as gender and age. To ensure the statistical significance of his results, he will calculate the statistical power of his sample based on confidence level and confidence interval before he finalises the exact size of his sample. However, Brian must first address two critical questions. First, how is he going to find so many patients? Second, even if he finds enough patients, how will he deal with ethical issues of anonymity and access to sensitive data? Brian is interested in learning the various methods in surveys to decide which method is the most appropriate for his own research.

Discuss

- How could Brian address these questions?
- Could a survey help Brian address his research question and help him deal with any ethical issues at the same time?

Methods in survey research

The most common types of methods that are widely used in survey research are face-to-face interviews, telephone interviews and mailed questionnaires. However, nowadays, online surveys are also an option (Kothari, 2004). For instance, when deciding on face-to-face interviews, the researcher has a major role in the output, since this depends on his/her ability to gather all the necessary information. Overall, this is a more structured way of collecting data (Kothari, 2004). Nevertheless, some of its major disadvantages are that it is costly and that a significant amount of time needs to be dedicated to training the interviewers. In addition, in the case of addressing sensitive issues, the accuracy of responses might be affected due to social desirability bias (The Health Communication Unit at the Centre for Health Promotion, 1999).

Written questionnaires, however, may be more than adequate if

- A homogeneous group is being studied.
- Mailing lists are available to eliminate sampling costs.
- Budgetary constraints are severe.
- Lower data quality is acceptable.

Personal interviews are best if

- Data quality is maximised.
- Cost is not an important consideration.

- The study involves a population that is difficult to reach otherwise.
- The population is geographically concentrated.

Combining data collection modes within a single study is another frequently used alternative. For example, a written questionnaire may be left with a respondent to be completed after a personal interview.

After the initial decisions to use a structured questionnaire and to use a particular data collection mode, a number of additional steps are involved in the research process:

1. Choosing specific content areas to be covered
2. Deciding to use existing scales or new items and how extensively to cover content areas
3. Deciding on item wording
4. Developing a questionnaire draft
5. Obtaining feedback from colleagues, revising the questionnaire
6. Pretesting using respondents from the same population and using actual interviewers.
7. Analysing pretest data and revising the questionnaire
8. Final interviewer training
9. Administering the final questionnaire
10. Coding and analysis of data

In the case of mailed questionnaires, questionnaires are mailed to the respondents, and then respondents return the questionnaires via mail. Still, there are some disadvantages, such as instances when the participants refuse to participate and the reasons for their refusal cannot be recorded. Furthermore, missing data is also an issue when it comes to mailed questionnaires.

Regarding the design of the questionnaire, the researcher should decide on the rationale behind each question they intend to ask, and decide whether the questions should be open-ended or closed-ended. Open-ended questions provide participants with the opportunity to speak more freely about the subject under investigation, whereas closed-ended questions are meant to be answered with a "yes" or "no" option. Moreover, the researcher should present a logical flow of the sections of the questionnaire in relation to the purpose of the interview. Special attention should be given to allocating a unique identification number to each questionnaire.

Indicative response formats could include rating scales, the best-known of these being the Likert scale, where responses range from 1 to 5, or vice versa, indicating agreement with a question; rankings, where the respondent orders his/her answer preference; and multiple choice questions, either choosing the most appropriate answer or giving a negative or positive response (Yates, 2004). In addition, there are also several types of measurements that could be used in relation to attitudes, knowledge, beliefs, behaviours and evaluations.

Prior to administering a questionnaire, it is essential to test the draft versions of the survey (Yates, 2004). The questionnaire should be written in simple language, asking only the necessary questions relating to the information that the researcher wishes to obtain; should involve the target groups and stakeholders in its design; should avoid double-barrelled questions and, finally, should be based on an extensive literature review. Next, it is also important for the researcher to consider the sample size, which should be large enough for the results to be generalisable and representative. So, in selecting the sample, the researcher should consider the size of the target population, the available budget and whether any subgroups would be needed (Bowling, 2014). There are several sampling techniques that could be used, including simple random samples, convenience samples, stratified random samples and cluster samples. Furthermore, there are a variety of sources available for obtaining a sample, such as phone books, CD-ROMS for phone listings and professional directories. To be more precise, in the case of conducting mail surveys, addresses and postal codes, as well as first and last names, should be obtained; in the case of telephone surveys, phone numbers with area codes would be needed and in the case of intercept surveys, representative locations would be required.

An important part of conducting surveys involves the training of the interviewers on reading the questions as written, not implying the response to the interviewee and clarifying questions without implying answers, for example, "Could you please elaborate further on that issue?" In addition, they should be able to probe for responses, for example, "Is there anything else you would like to add?" Recording answers is also essential, and this could be done by recording them verbatim on a piece of paper and then copying the responses to the questionnaire upon completion of the interview to document all the information given by the interviewee.

The interviewer should show that he or she understands that the interviewee's time is valuable and make it clear that the opinions of the interviewee are essential to the study. Furthermore, in the case that the survey needs to be stopped for any reason, the interviewer should arrange another appointment with the interviewee in order to complete the survey. In the case that an individual refuses to take part in the survey, the interviewer should respect the person's right to decline to participate and, in a polite manner, try to obtain the reason for their refusal. For instance, if they are busy at that time, the interview could be scheduled for a more suitable time. If they are concerned about the nature of the study, a more detailed description should be provided to them. Reassurance about the confidentiality of the information given should be provided throughout the whole process. In all cases, the interviewer should be polite and consider all the ethical factors.

Another important aspect of conducting surveys is to record the appointments with any potential participant, as well as the reasons for refusal, in order to have control over the data. This could be enhanced through the development of an Excel sheet or a simple Word table, in which a code should be given to each potential participant, followed by their phone numbers and their demographics as well as the time of the interview. In the case of rescheduling, the new date and time should be given with brief notes in relation to the reasons why the interview was cancelled, together with notes on their verbal and non-verbal communication throughout the interview.

To ensure the integrity of the information collected, the researcher should describe the way that the data were collected via the different survey methods. More specifically, when the researcher aims to collect data via face-to-face interviews, the first thing that should be taken into consideration is the interview venue; it is up to the interviewer to decide where he or she feels most comfortable with providing information about the survey. In the case of an intercept survey, more than one location should be used to ensure a better representation of the population. In the case that a specific group is needed for the survey, it is suggested to first develop a questionnaire screener in order to find eligible participants. In other words, the researcher could screen for demographics to identify their eligibility. In the case that the participants are not eligible for the interview, the interview is brought to an end after the screening questions. Finally, supervision of the interviewers is imperative in the case that a telephone survey is to be conducted to ensure that they are following the interviewing protocol. A follow-up in relation to the actual completion of the interview should also be conducted (The Health Communication Unit at the Centre for Health Promotion, 1999).

In conclusion, a thorough assessment (see Table 2.1) of the most appropriate survey method to be used must be conducted in relation to the method that will return the highest response rate, will be more convenient to the researcher, will be within the timeline, will be cost-effective and will be suitable for the staff and resources available.

Brian is pleased with the information he has so far about using cross-sectional social survey as an appropriate method for addressing his research questions. He has started considering the mail survey as a possible choice, as it has some advantages for his research and study population. First, he can mail questionnaires to as many patients as he can locate. Second, Brian can deal with ethical concerns as well, since he will not have direct contact with the patients. He could come to an agreement with departments or agencies that control the diabetes registry, which could mail the questionnaires to the patients on his behalf. Brian could prepare a covering note, which would inform the patients about the study and the questionnaire. If there is no diabetes registry, Brian could send the questionnaires either through hospitals' lists or via patients' groups. What Brian is now concerned with is the relatively low response rate usually associated with a mail survey.

Discuss

- What is the response rate of mail surveys? Does it vary? Why?
- What could Brian do to maximise the response rate of his study?

The response rate for mail surveys can vary considerably. Schutt (2004) explained that a response rate of 30 per cent or 60 per cent might not be useful, because the

Table 2.1 Different types of interviews: Advantages and disadvantages

Type of Interview	*Characteristics*	*Strengths*	*Weaknesses*
(1) Informal conversational interview	Questions emerge from the immediate context and are asked in the natural course of things; there is no predetermination of question topics or wording.	Increases the salience and relevance of questions; interview is built on and emerges from observations; the interview can be matched to individuals and circumstances.	Different information collected from different people with different questions. Less systematic and comprehensive if certain questions do not arise "naturally". Data organisation and analysis can be quite difficult.
(2) Interview guide approach	Topics and issues to be covered are specified in advance, in outline form; interviewer decides sequence and wording of questions in the course of the interview.	The outline increases the comprehensiveness of the data and makes data collection somewhat systematic for each respondent. Logical gaps in data can be anticipated and closed. Interviews remain fairly conversational and situational.	Important and salient topics may be inadvertently omitted. Interviewer flexibility in sequencing and wording questions can result in substantially different responses, thus reducing the comparability of responses.
(3) Standardized open-ended interview	The exact wording and sequence of questions are determined in advance. All interviewees are asked the same basic questions in the same order.	Respondents answer the same questions, thus increasing comparability of responses; data are complete for each person on the topics addressed in the interview. Reduces interviewer effects and bias when several interviewers are used. Permits decision makers to see and review the instrumentation used in the evaluation. Facilitates organisation and analysis of the data.	Little flexibility in relating the interview to particular individuals and circumstances; standardised wording of questions may constrain and limit naturalness and relevance of questions and answers.

validity of results would be in jeopardy. However, Schutt further stressed that a response rate of 70 per cent or higher can result in more robust findings, and there are ways to achieve it. For example, a covering note that provides a brief but at the same time a detailed explanation about the importance of the survey, as well as the procedures, is imperative. Then, the researcher should send out the first mailing, followed by a reminder card to remind individuals of the importance of the survey as well as the importance of their contribution. A second mailing should be sent 3 to 4 weeks later, emphasising the importance of receiving responses and enclosing a new questionnaire and return envelope to further increase the response rate (Schutt, 2004). The response rate could be further increased by enclosing a self-addressed, stamped envelope and by writing a letter in a personalised form. Further, the questionnaire should be kept as short as possible, and questions should be pre-coded to facilitate the responses. Another idea is a combination of survey methods; for example, mailing the questionnaire and then following up with non-respondents via a telephone interview (The Health Communication Unit at the Centre for Health Promotion, 1999).

Brian is even more confident now that a mail survey can be a useful method for addressing his research question, as it can help him study all the parameters he wants to explore, address ethical issues and increase the number of participants as much as possible. The next issue Brian should address is processing the data in a manner that will lead to their best use.

Analysis of survey data

To code data, the researcher should familiarise himself or herself with the questionnaire and topic area, create two groups with a distinct code list for open-ended questions and prepare a draft code list by reading at least 15 per cent of the questionnaires and isolating all the unique responses. In the case that no new responses are found, the researcher should rewrite the codes and assign a number to each code. As far as the data entry is concerned, there are two methods: direct data entry, where upon completion of the questionnaire the data are coded and entered into software for analysis, and computer assisted telephone interviewing (CATI), where responses are directly inputted into a computer and the questions requiring coding are entered at a different time. It is also important to verify the data entered to increase confidence in the accuracy of the data. This could be achieved through programming data entry to check each field for out-of-range data in order to identify errors and inconsistencies, providing an ID number to the record counterpart in the questionnaire and identifying the source of error to enter the corrected data (The Health Communication Unit at the Centre for Health Promotion, 1999).

In the case that a computer is not available, it is impossible to analyse the large amount of data by hand. Therefore, it is strongly recommended to use statistical software such as the Statistical Package for the Social Sciences (SPSS) or to enter data into Excel. SPSS provides a large number of statistical and mathematical functions, scores of statistical procedures and a very flexible data handling capability, and can read data in almost any format (e.g. numeric, alphanumeric, binary, dollar, date, time etc.). As far as data analysis is concerned, factors have been identified in the literature that affect the way data are analysed, including the number of variables being examined, the level of measurement of the variables and whether the researcher wants to use the data for descriptive or inferential purposes (de Vaus, 1991). Thus, data analysis depends on the number of variables. For example, if the researcher wants to analyse one characteristic of the sample at a time (e.g. sex, vote, income level), the researcher will use a univariate (one-variable) method of analysis. In the case that the researcher wants to analyse two variables at a time, he or she will use a bivariate (two-variable) method (e.g. if the researcher wants to see whether women vote differently than men) (de Vaus, 1991). Multiple linear regression could also be used to investigate all questions related to two-variable relationships and group comparisons. Multiple linear regression is a data analysis strategy with several independent variables and one dependent variable, which aims to account for variance in the dependent variable (Punch, 2005).

A multivariate technique will be used in the event that the researcher wants to investigate a research question that makes use of three or more variables, but he or she first needs to specify the conceptual status of the variables in the survey (e.g. some as independent, some as control variables or covariates, and some as dependent) in line with the research questions (de Vaus, 1991). An advantage of this technique is that it forces the researcher to be specific in formulating research questions and in translating them into data analysis operations (Punch, 2005). It is essential, before one analyses data, to clarify the research question that will guide the analysis. It is a common phenomenon to develop and refine a question in the process of analysis, so one usually moves between univariate, bivariate and multivariate techniques (de Vaus, 1991).

After deciding what type of analysis to use, the researcher needs to decide which technique to use within these broad categories. A factor that needs to be taken in account when deciding is the level of measurement of the variables being used and the way that categories of the variable relate to one another. Three levels of measurement exist: nominal, ordinal and interval/ratio. A nominal variable is defined as one where the researcher can distinguish between categories of a variable but cannot rank the categories in any order (e.g. place of birth, sex and marital status). An ordinal variable is one where it is meaningful to rank the categories. In other words, an ordinal variable constitutes any variable in which categories can be ranked but where the difference between the categories cannot be quantified in precise numerical terms (de Vaus, 1991). An interval/ratio variable is one in which the categories have a natural ranking and it is possible to quantify precisely the differences between the categories (e.g. age could be an interval variable if it is measured in years, since precise differences between ages can be quantified). In the case that age was measured as young, middle-aged and old, it could be an ordinal variable (de Vaus, 1991).

As far as the level of measurement is concerned, this can be determined by the researcher via the format of the question and response categories, how the question is coded and through its application (de Vaus, 1991). For example, if the researcher asks a participant how much paid work they have done and "none", "part time" and "full time" are stated as response categories, the variable will be ordinal. If the researcher asks how many hours per week a participant works, the variable will be interval. If the researcher asks how many hours per week the participant works and provides the responses "none", "1–10", "11–20", "21–30", "31–40" and "40 plus", this will be an ordinal variable (de Vaus, 1991). As far as the application of the variables is concerned, there are situations in which it is the rule to rank the categories of a variable (e.g. treating it as ordinal) and there are situations in which it would be meaningless to rank them.

Next, the researcher needs to consider which level of measurement to aim for. The researcher needs to take into consideration that there is a wide range of methods of analysis considered to be appropriate as the level of measurement of variables increases. Interval-level variables require more powerful and sophisticated techniques (higher levels of measurement provide more information, but the researcher needs to consider whether they are necessary). In addition, questions that require a lot of precision and detail can be unreliable, since people often do not provide accurate, detailed information. There are also times when participants will be reluctant to provide precise information but may provide it in more general terms (e.g. income bracket, age cohort). In addition, numerical data collected in grouped form (e.g. age, income categories) can be converted to interval data if the researcher makes assumptions. Also, if the variables are measured at an interval level, it is simple to reduce them to the ordinal or nominal level (de Vaus, 1991).

Data analysis could be achieved through descriptive statistics (frequencies, means and ranges) or through comparisons between subgroups of the population or from measurements taken at different times. Descriptive statistics are those that summarise patterns in the responses of people in the sample (de Vaus, 1991). Techniques that could be used are means, standard deviations and frequency distributions. In the case that scales are involved, item analysis could be used (Punch, 2005). Initial descriptive analysis keeps the researcher close to the data and helps him or her to understand the distribution of each variable across the survey respondents (Punch, 2005).

Alternatively, inferential statistics help the researcher gain an idea of whether the patterns described in the sample are likely to apply in the population from which the sample is drawn (de Vaus, 1991). The inference question should be: How likely am I to be wrong if I infer that what I found to be true of my sample is also true of my population? The answers should be formed as "times per 100" or "times per 1000". This leads to statements such as "I would be wrong fewer than 5 times per 100 if I make the inference" (or fewer than 5 times in 1000). These could be statistical significance levels, confidence levels or probability levels, usually presented as $p < 0.05$ or $p < 0.01$. Statistical significance levels are useful in guiding researchers' decisions about whether results are real or not. In order to work out the likelihood of being wrong, the researcher needs to calculate some statistics from the sample data and then use statistical inference tables to determine that likelihood: for example, chi-square, comparing observed and expected distributions, or r, showing the level of association between variables, or F, comparing the predictive efficiency of two regression models. Then, the researcher refers that statistic to its distribution as shown in statistical inference tables in order to see how likely it is that a value of that size would be obtained for this statistic by chance (Punch, 2005).

Thus, the researcher should interpret the survey findings through statistical tests, as well as in discussions with stakeholders, having in mind the survey's aims and organising them in relation to the research questions. The survey findings should be interpreted in accordance with the aim of the project, bearing the audience in mind when drafting the report, while also taking into consideration the limitations of the survey and possible biases (selection, non-response, measurement etc.). Moreover, the researcher should consider the validity and reliability of the results while also considering their generalisability. When presenting the findings, the researcher should pay attention to the research questions and only present the information that answers those questions; select a format that will highlight the key results; simplify the presentation of interpretation and present it in tables, images, graphs, pie charts and so on (Bowling, 2014).

Last but not least, the researcher should be in a position to provide implications for further research and practice by involving the stakeholders in interpreting the findings; revisiting the original goals of data collection; writing a list of recommendations in relation to the survey outcomes; ranking the changes that need to be made in relation to their feasibility; preparing an action plan to implement the recommended changes and implementing the changes.

Advantages and disadvantages of conducting social surveys

As with any other research method, there are some advantages and disadvantages to conducting social surveys. Specifically, surveys can help in completing structured questionnaires with many stakeholders in a short timeframe and can be completed in various forms (e-mail, telephone, mail and face-to-face). If sampling is allocated with caution (i.e. in a generalised and standardised manner), structured questionnaires may minimise interviewer's bias. Finally, data analysis is time effective as compared with qualitative data analysis, and social surveys are socially versatile, since they can be used by a variety of professions. On the other hand, the disadvantages of social surveys relate to financial resources, since they can be costly, and to the capacity and skills of the researcher in terms of statistical analysis and the interpretation of the findings.

Conclusion

This chapter presented the basic features of the social survey and how it could be useful in addressing Brian's research questions. Surveys are useful for collecting data from a large number of participants, and they mainly elicit quantitative results that can be coded and analysed through statistical software. Despite their limitations, surveys are used in many studies, while a mail survey can be a useful way to study a large sample while dealing with issues of anonymity and sensitivity.

References

Adal E, Önal Z, Ersen A, Yalçın K, Önal H and Aydın A. (2015) Recognizing the psychosocial aspects of type 1 diabetes in adolescents. *Journal of Clinical Research in Pediatric Endocrinology* 7(1): 57–62.

Bowling A (2014) *Research Methods in Health: Investigating Health and Health services* (4th ed.). Berkshire: McGraw-Hill.

de Vaus D (1991) *Surveys in Social Research*. London: Routledge.

Gucciardi E, Wang SCT, DeMelo M, Amaral L and Stewart DE (2008) Characteristics of men and women with diabetes. Observations during patients' initial visit to a diabetes education centre. *Canadian Family Physician* 54(2): 219–227.

Hakim C (1987) *Research Design. Strategies and Choices in the Design of Social Research*. London: Routledge.

Hapunda G, Abubakar A, van de Vijver F and Pouwer F (2015) Living with type 1 diabetes is challenging for Zambian adolescents: Qualitative data on stress, coping with stress and quality of care and life. *BMC Endocrine Disorders* 15(1): 20.

Irani MD, Abdoli S, Bijan I, Parvizy S, Fatemi NS and Amini M (2014) Strategies to overcome type 1 diabetes–related social stigma in the Iranian society. *Iranian Journal of Nursing and Midwifery Research* 19(5): 456.

Kothari CR (2004) *Research Methodology. Methods and Techniques* (2nd ed.). New Delhi: New Age International Publishers.

Li J, Drury V and Taylor B (2013) 'Diabetes is nothing': The experience of older Singaporean women living and coping with type 2 diabetes. *Contemporary Nurse* 45(2): 188–196.

Mathew R, Gucciardi E, De Melo M and Barata P (2012) Self-management experiences among men and women with type 2 diabetes mellitus: A qualitative analysis. *BMC Family Practice* 13(1): 122.

NICE Guideline (2006) Diabetes Mellitus. Available online at: http://www.nice.org.uk/guidance/TA113. Accessed 21 December 2015.

Nicolucci A, Kovacs Burns K, Holt RIG, Comaschi M, Hermanns N, Ishii H, Kokoszka A, Pouwer F, Skovlund SE, Stukey H, Tarkun I, Vallis M, Wens J and Peyrot, M (2013) Diabetes Attitudes, Wishes and Needs second study (DAWN2™): Cross national benchmarking of diabetes related psychosocial outcomes for people with diabetes. *Diabetic Medicine* 30(7): 767–777.

Protudjer JL, Dumontet J and McGavock JM (2014) My voice: A grounded theory analysis of the lived experience of type 2 diabetes in adolescence. *Canadian Journal of Diabetes* 38(4): 229–236.

Punch KF (2005) *Introduction to Social Research: Quantitative and Qualitative Approaches*. London: SAGE.

Rubin RR, Peyrot M and Siminerio LM (2006) Health care and patient-reported outcomes: Results of the cross-national Diabetes Attitudes, Wishes and Needs (DAWN) study. *Diabetes Care* 29: 1249–1255.

Schutt RK (2004) *Investigating the Social World* (4th ed.). London: Pine Forge Press.

Sriram V, Sridhar GR and Madhu K (2005) Gender and diabetes. *Journal of Health Social Behaviour* 21(2): 97–102.

The Health Communication Unit at the Centre for Health Promotion (1999). Conducting Survey Research. Available online at: http://gradnyc.com/wp-content/uploads/2012/08/GNYC_Academy_Workshop-3_Conducting-Survey-Research.pdf. Accessed 18 January 2016.

Visser PS, Krosnick JA and Lavrakas PJ (2000) Survey research. In: Reis HT and Judd CM (eds) *Handbook of Research Methods in Social and Personality Psychology*. New York: Cambridge University Press.

Yates SJ (2004) *Doing Social Research*. London: SAGE.

3 Qualitative interviews

Thalassaemia

Abstract

Dr Andrew Stefanides is relocating to the thalassaemia clinic in Nicosia, Cyprus. In the past, thalassaemia was quite prominent across the island, and about one in seven people has the thalassaemia gene. Dr Stefanides has read a few research articles about the quality of life of people with thalassaemia and learned that the patients' quality of life is worse than that of healthy individuals. However, Dr Stefanides could not understand why this was the case, since people with thalassaemia can be socially active like everyone else. He is, therefore, interested in finding out about ways to explore the experiences of thalassaemia patients.

This chapter focuses on thalassaemia and its impact on the patients' lives. It discusses how thalassaemia is a social experience and applies the research method of qualitative, in-depth interviews in order to explore the experience of living with thalassaemia and to go into greater depth as to what patients go through and how their quality of life deteriorates.

Learning objectives:

- Describe the main research findings on how patients experience thalassaemia.
- Explain the main features of qualitative in-depth interviews.
- Outline the principles of asking questions.
- Describe how data saturation is reached and how coding is carried out.

Scenario

Dr Andrew Stefanides, a haematologist, has been working in London with patients who have been diagnosed with sickle cell disease and thalassaemia for more than 10 years. He decides to move to Cyprus and work at the Thalassaemia Department in Nicosia. Thalassaemia is an inherited blood disorder caused when two people who both possess the thalassaemia mutation have children. Treatments involve systematic blood transfusion and iron-chelation therapy. Thalassaemia disease is quite common in Mediterranean countries, and Cyprus has one of the highest rates of thalassaemia carriers – one in seven people has the mutation, a ratio that escalates the chances of having children with the disease. Consequently, Andrew's knowledge and experience will be beneficial for both the patients in Nicosia and other healthcare professionals who work with patients with Thalassemia.

Before moving to Cyprus, Andrew reads through the relevant literature with regard to the quality of life of thalassaemia patients in order to learn as much as possible about what patients experience. Through the relevant literature, Andrew learns that studies that measured patients' quality of life found that patients with thalassaemia generally had a worse quality of life compared with healthy people. Specifically, their lives were socially restricted (especially due to iron-chelation therapy), their life expectancy was significantly lower and they experienced stigmatisation. After reading this basic scientific information Andrew is puzzled, as he cannot understand why people with thalassaemia suffer from a worse quality of life, since many of them are employed and have families. He tries to find more information through the quantitative studies he reads; however, he does not manage to learn much.

Discuss

- Why did Andrew not manage to find out more about the reasons why patients with thalassaemia have a poor quality of life?
- Why could quantitative studies not provide answers?
- What could Andrew do to find answers to his questions?

Andrew looks into the literature once more in order to understand why patients with thalassaemia experience a poorer quality of life. He also develops an interest in identifying how his patients in Cyprus experience thalassaemia. However, he is uncertain how to proceed in order to examine his interests and report back on his potential findings.

Social aspects of thalassaemia disease

There is evidence to suggest that the illness experience of thalassaemia is a multidimensional one, because patients are born with the disease and, thus, it is part of their identity. Despite this, while growing up, they find themselves having to deal with psychological and social challenges. More specifically, Hatzouli (2012) found that, in Greece, patients with thalassaemia constantly renegotiate their self-image. On the one hand, they feel abnormal. On the other hand, they feel that they have contributed to the development of modern bio-medicine, which has helped patients with thalassaemia to live as normal a life as possible. Moreover, Hatzouli explained that her participants felt stigmatised and socially isolated. As a result, some of her participants opted to hide their condition in order to avoid dealing with the social stigma attached to the disease. One of the most challenging aspects of thalassaemia, according to Hatzouli's participants, was treatment itself, since patients had to have frequent blood transfusions and chelation therapy. A quantitative study by Telfer *et al.* (2009) revealed that patients in Cyprus considered that their quality of life was affected negatively because of the life-long treatment, being different and experiencing delayed sexual development, as well as side effects and uncertainty. Gollo *et al.*'s (2013) research in Italy found similar results: patients with thalassemia had a low quality of life as compared with their healthier counterparts. Interestingly, Gollo *et al.*'s research was longitudinal and highlighted that advancements in therapies between 2001 and 2009 resulted in a significant improvement in the patients' quality of life.

Due to low life expectancy, which has recently been estimated to be 50 years (Tefler, 2009), other studies focused largely on adolescents and identified similar results as the studies outlined above. Gharaibeh *et al.* (2009) conducted a quantitative study of patients from 6 to 18 years old to identify the psychosocial burden of thalassaemia disease. The study showed an important relationship between having thalassaemia and gender and education. More specifically, thalassaemia and the need for blood transfusion had a negative impact on school attendance. Interestingly, male patients noted more negative experiences due to the greater social pressure exerted on them to have more responsibilities (i.e. work) compared with female patients. Regardless of gender, when patients suffered from complications, they started feeling they were different from healthy people. Along similar lines, a comparative study in 10 countries found that thalassaemia had a negative impact on patients' social life and that patients felt different because they thought that it was not acceptable for them to have children (Caro *et al.*, 2002). Interestingly, a quantitative study of patients between 5 and 18 years old by Yalcin *et al.* (2007) indicated that older patients were less likely than younger patients to have problems when thinking about the disease. Sherman *et al.* (1985) shed some light on the reason why older adolescent patients had a better understanding of their disease. In their study of 23 patients between 6 and 16 years old, they found that parents of older children were open to discussing the disease with their children, whereas parents of younger children were more guarded, possibly to protect them. This parental approach caused older children to have a better understanding of the disease, while the younger patients were more confused about it.

A descriptive and explanatory research study of 36 patients between 9 and 17 years old conducted by Roy and Chatterjee (2007) revealed similar trends. That is, patients described their treatment as exhausting, and they considered themselves to be a burden. Given this, some patients avoided treatment, placing themselves at risk of experiencing complications. Moreover, their school attendance was poor, and travelling to the hospital for blood transfusions interfered with their social life. Finally, some children felt that they would lose their friends due to having an incurable disease.

Qualitative studies demonstrated similar results but went more deeply into the patients' experiences. More specifically, William *et al.* (2009: 1446) interviewed 32 children and young people with cystic fibrosis in Scotland. Cystic fibrosis is not a blood disorder like thalassaemia, but it is a genetic disease; therefore, as with thalassaemia, people are born with it, and thus their lives are not disrupted due to the sudden diagnosis of a chronic condition. The authors found that, in general, children with cystic fibrosis did not experience biographical disruption. Interestingly, biographical disruption was present but in a more hidden way. More specifically, the authors observed what they called "normalities": children understood themselves as first, "normal to the self", which relates to accepting one's condition as normal; second, "normal for self", which means that children did things in order to feel normal; third, "normal to other", whereby children wanted other people to view their condition as normal; fourth, "normal for other", in the sense that children did things in order to prove to others that they were normal.

A recent qualitative study of the experience of thalassaemia in Cyprus, presented at the European Association of Social Anthropologists conference, showed that adults with thalassaemia experience "biographical unfulfilment" even though they have achieved basic cultural goals, such as having a family, completing higher education and being employed (Constantinou *et al.*, 2014). This is because patients thought that they could achieve more if they did not have thalassaemia. Interestingly, this qualitative study in Cyprus revealed similar results as William *et al.*'s study of cystic fibrosis in the sense that, when participants from Cyprus were asked to express their experiences as children, they said that they regarded themselves as normal and that they did things to convince themselves and others that they were normal.

The impact of thalassaemia is not confined solely to patients; rather, it extends to encompass the parents of children with thalassaemia, who experience psychosocial issues as well. More specifically, Prasomsuk *et al.* (2007) interviewed 15 mothers of children with Thalassemia. They found that the mothers felt that they needed to know more about the disease, they experienced psychosocial problems such as sadness, their children's school attendance was poor, and they faced financial difficulties due to the need to travel regularly to the hospital for blood transfusion. At the same time, they were concerned about the future due to fear of complications and death. An earlier study of adolescents between 13 and 19 years old by Georganda (1988) had shown that parents were careful regarding whom they talked to about their children's disease because they did not want to lose friends due to thalassaemia. Furthermore, parents' major concerns had to do with the fear of death and health complications. The adolescents in this study said that using a pump for chelation therapy was the most difficult part of the treatment because it was painful and it constantly reminded them of having thalassaemia.

The qualitative studies above helped Andrew realise that quantitative research presents figures and tends to provide an overall picture. Research, interestingly, needs to rely on qualitative studies in order to explore topics in greater depth, given that qualitative methods analyse words, not numbers. This means that researchers should not view people as numbers but, rather, should spend time talking to them as well. Andrew realises that in-depth interviewing can inform him more thoroughly about the reasons why patients with thalassaemia go through what they go through. Andrew wants to acquire such knowledge about patients with thalassaemia in Cyprus, where he will be practising over the next few years. Andrew starts noting down a few interview questions on paper, but he is not sure how he should proceed. Should he only ask questions that he has listed in his interview guide? How long should each interview take? How can he document the answers? How should he analyse the interviews? These are some of the questions that concern him.

Discuss

- What are the steps that a researcher must take in qualitative research?
- How should interviews be carried out?
- Are there any difficulties in phrasing and asking questions?
- How can an interviewee's responses be analysed effectively?

In-depth qualitative interviews

In qualitative research, the approach to issues or topics is different from the one employed in quantitative methods. In quantitative research methodology, research usually starts with a research hypothesis and, consequently, researchers collect data in order to accept or reject the initial hypothesis (Bryman, 2001). In qualitative research, however, researchers may start with more general questions or areas of interest, collect data, make sense of it, come up with theoretical frameworks or concepts, collect additional data and interpret this further. This process is inductive in the sense that researchers are producing theory from the data (Bowling, 2014). A researcher who decides to use interviews would possibly have a more generic research question; for example, "how do in-patients construct new social networks in hospitals?" Interviews, therefore, largely explore "how is happening" and "why is happening" research questions rather than "what is happening" queries, which are mainly answered by quantitative research. Given this, and having reviewed the general literature on the social aspects of thalassaemia, Andrew puts forward a general research question as follows: "What is the impact of thalassaemia disease on patients' social life and identity?" Andrew may refine his research question based on new information from the literature and just before he starts interviewing his patients. Andrew will rely on a "general inductive approach" (Thomas, 2006) for conducting, coding and analysing the interviews. The general inductive approach focuses on the most important meanings in a text rather than generating theory (grounded theory) or exploring people's conscious experiences and behaviour (phenomenology).

There are several types of interviews. Interviews can be structured, semi-structured and unstructured. Structured interviews often involve fixed questions without any room for asking more questions during the interview (Bryman, 2001). Semi-structured interviews are more flexible. Researchers create a list of questions, which are focused on the topic or the research question they are exploring, but they allow room for posing more questions should they arise over the course of the interview. For example, to the question "Has your life changed in any way after being diagnosed with diabetes?" a patient may answer "No, it hasn't. I just stay at home more now." This statement answers the question, but a mindful researcher should further question the second part of the response and ask for the reasons why the patient stays home more often now or what the patient used to do before the diagnosis that he or she cannot or does not want to do any longer. In unstructured interviews, researchers do not have any specific questions but, rather, only areas of interest; thus, researchers formulate the questions during the interview. This allows even more flexibility, because participants are not responding to specific frames of inquiry but are left to reflect on certain areas more freely. Andrew decides that in order to explore the research question "What is the impact of thalassaemia disease on patients' social life and identity?" semi-structured interviews are more appropriate, because he can formulate questions based on the existing studies and allow room for more questions, which will be specific to his patients.

Discuss

- What questions should Andrew prepare?
- Is there anything he should do to prepare for the interviews?

Andrew can start preparing questions through two main sources. First, through his own experiences with patients with inherited blood disorders, Andrew can think of possible questions that pertain to what patients have gone through since they realised what the treatment of their disease involved "and how that affected their job career later in their life". Relying on his own experiences is very important for Andrew's research, because what he has gathered from his own patients may be quite unique in that it has not yet been researched or documented by others. Second, Andrew should revisit the relevant literature and make notes of the main topics that derive from published research findings. Andrew could then turn these topics into specific questions to include in his interview guide. Andrew could rely on Bryman's (2001: 317–318) suggestion that an interview guide should consist of specific steps: (1) order the questions to ensure good flow, (2) focus questions on the topic under investigation, (3) write the questions in a simple way, (4) avoid leading questions, (5) ask about demographic characteristics, (6) learn more about the conditions under which participants live and work, (7) record the interviews and (8) ensure that the interview takes place somewhere participants feel comfortable and where a discussion can take place without interruptions.

Interestingly, following Bryman's interview guide would not suffice in order to conduct the interviews in a scientific and objective way. During the interview, Andrew should demonstrate the capabilities outlined by Kvale in 1996 (cited in Bryman, 2001: 318). That is, he should have knowledge and experience of interviewing; he should structure the interview carefully, ask clear questions, have a plan and be kind, sensitive and critical, as well as being able to recall and clarify what is being said. Andrew would certainly need to undertake additional reading on how to conduct interviews and perhaps go through a relevant training session before starting his research.

Asking questions

One of the key elements of interviewing is asking questions, which refers to the types of questions asked, the sequence and the actual phrasing. In interviews, researchers may use closed questions to gather some factual information, but, typically, open questions (questions that allow interviewees to answer openly without the need to choose an answer from a list) dominate the interview guide. Open questions also help to establish a good rapport with research participants because they are given the opportunity to talk about their experiences – they feel that their experiences are heard and thus are important (Silverman *et al*., 2013).

Andrew needs to pay particular attention to formulating focused and simple open questions to learn as much as possible from his research participants. Asking questions in interviews is not very different from asking questions in closed questionnaires in the sense that questions should be simple and researchers should avoid asking two things at the same time or including double negatives. Doing so would only confuse participants and would hinder them from providing researchers with focused and complete answers. Another type of question that Andrew should avoid is the leading question. A leading question is one that leads to a desired answer; for example, "You feel pain, don't you?" However, leading questions could be subtler than this example, and researchers should be very careful and well trained to avoid them. The question "What life changes did you experience since you developed osteoarthritis?" is a leading question, because it leads the interviewee to talk about changes even though he or she may never have experienced any changes. The correct way to go about this would be to start with a more general question, such as "Have you experienced any changes in your life since you developed osteoarthritis?" If the interviewee says "yes" or outlines a few, a more specific question about the changes the interviewee has experienced could follow. Andrew can deal with this challenge either by undergoing relevant training or by piloting his skills. For example, he could lead an interview, record it, have it evaluated by an experienced colleague and then self-reflect on how it went.

Since Andrew has decided to use semi-structured interviewing, he must be prepared to ask more questions than planned or to pose questions in order to have things clarified or elaborated on. This is called "probing" and is quite common in interviews. There are various ways to probe effectively. Bernard (1995) asserted that researchers can just ask respondents to clarify a point, they can remain silent (interviewees may understand this as a hint to continue) or they can summarise what the interviewee has said and then ask him or her to elaborate. Probing could also be set as a ground rule. For example, before starting interviews, researchers could inform participants that providing thorough answers would benefit the research. Setting such a ground rule from the onset makes it more likely that the interviewee will understand and accept probing questions during the interview.

Discuss

- How should Andrew select his participants?
- When should he stop? How many interviews should he conduct?

Sampling and data saturation

Andrew is concerned with the number of interviews he should be doing. Initially, he thinks that sampling in qualitative research is an endless matter and is worried.

Thus, he turns to the existing literature to learn more about it. He finds out that there are various types of qualitative sampling methods and that there is an end to the road (Schutt, 2004). First, purposive sampling is a method whereby participants are selected based on specific characteristics they have that are relevant to the research topic. This is used when researchers want to explore people with specific characteristics that are not typical of people from the general population (e.g. single parents with HIV). Second, convenient sampling refers to a process of selecting participants who are easily accessible. It is used quite often for the researchers' convenience or when it is difficult to locate potential participants elsewhere (e.g. interviewing people with HIV who visit a specific specialised clinic instead of looking for them in the general population). Third, snowball sampling is a method of finding potential participants with the help of other participants. This is used when researchers have difficulties finding participants on their own (i.e. interviewing young, homosexual men in a highly conservative community). In this way, researchers can find a couple of participants and ask them if they know other people who might be interested in participating in the project.

Andrew opts to use convenient sampling, as he will be interviewing patients at the department where he will be working. Thus, patients are easy to locate. If Andrew cannot find enough patients who are willing to participate, he may also employ the snowball method by asking his existing informants to let him know about any other potential research participants. Still, Andrew is puzzled: "When shall I stop?"

When to stop with sampling is an important issue in qualitative research as well as a challenging decision. Most researchers of published qualitative work said that they decided to stop sampling when saturation was reached. Practically speaking, what does this mean? Interestingly, there are only a few guidelines in the literature regarding how saturation is measured and eventually reached. Saturation "is reached when the researcher gathers data to the point of diminishing returns, when nothing new is being added" (Bowen, 2008: 140). However, the point "where nothing new is added" has not been adequately addressed. Reviewing the relevant literature, Guest *et al.* (2006) found only seven sources that provided some guidelines. Different scholars suggest different sample sizes, such as 36 or 15 or 6 interviews depending on the type of study and its theoretical basis. Morse (2000: 3–4) explained that saturation may be influenced by many factors. First, it depends on the "scope of the study". That is, a study with a narrow focus would need fewer informants. Second, the "nature of the topic" may have an impact if the topic is difficult and informants have reservations about expressing themselves. This links to the third factor, which pertains to the "quality of data", meaning that some informants may not provide researchers with detailed and relevant information. In this case, researchers may consider expanding their sample size. Fourth is the "study design" factor, whereby, for example, longitudinal studies, in contrast with non-longitudinal studies, will need more interviews. Morse outlined a fifth factor, which she called "shadowed data". Shadowed data refers to information mentioned by participants that relates to other people rather than to the participants themselves. Morse considered this very important information because it gives an idea of the breadth of relevant information and thus an indication of the need to expand sample size.

Four guidelines about the saturation of data in qualitative interviews have been published. Bowen (2008) started with 26 interviews and added an additional 12 interviews after he relied on a constant comparison between concepts, code and data. He used Atlas Ti software and took notes, which he used later on to revise all the codes and concepts and to make sure that any gaps were filled. This relates mostly to the process of refining any concepts or codes. Bowen then gave us a numerical guide to saturation based on his own study. That is, he achieved saturation when codes or themes could be observed in more than 70 per cent of the interviews. However, Bowen clarified that this number should not be used in isolation; rather, researchers should consider other parameters. More specifically, they should cross-check the codes with comments from participants relating to the coded data, while the data should agree with information acquired from key informants before commencing research.

Guest *et al.* (2006) came up with a more detailed procedure. In their study of people who were at risk of being infected with HIV, they conducted 30 interviews with people from Ghana and 30 with people from Nigeria. After coding all the interviews from Ghana, they came up with a codebook that contained 109 codes derived from the data. Seventy-three percent (80 codes) of these codes were identified in the first six interviews, while 20 more codes were observed in the next six interviews. The remaining nine codes did not come up as often as the others. No substantial additions were made when data from the Nigerian interviews were coded. In this case, Guest *et al.* (2006) reached saturation with 12 interviews. Though this number may be only specific to Guest *et al.*'s study, the authors provided us with a methodology of checking for data saturation.

Francis *et al.* (2010) recommended an initial sampling of 10 interviews. They studied medical practitioners' beliefs about how to manage patients with sore throat. To check for data saturation, they decided to include only beliefs shared by at least two participants. When they reached zero shared beliefs, they applied a plus-three interviews criterion. If there continued to be zero shared beliefs for another three interviews, they concluded that they had reached data saturation.

A fourth methodology has been recently published by Constantinou *et al.* (2017) called CoMeTS (Comparative Method for Themes Saturation). CoMeTS is holistic in the sense that all words from research participants are coded and counted for saturation. The construction of themes starts from the first interview, and all interviews are compared with each until saturation is achieved. Constantinou *et al.* also found order-induced error, which occurs because of the sequence of interviews that are coded and checked for saturation. Due to the small number of interviews in qualitative research, the majority of themes may be concentrated in the first interviews of the sequence. Therefore, Constantinou *et al.* suggested reordering the sequence multiple times and checking for saturation again in order to ensure that saturation is indeed achieved within the existing dataset.

Guest *et al.* (2006) explained that saturation has been considered as the "gold standard" for validity in qualitative health science research. Andrew takes achieving saturation very seriously and decides to take into account the influential factors identified by Morse (2000) and use the CoMeTS method for checking data saturation in order to make sure that he will have robust data. More specifically,

Andrew wants to keep the scope of his research broad but at the same time focused on patients' experiences that relate directly to thalassaemia. Moreover, in order to differentiate his research from existing research in Cyprus, Andrew wants to narrow his focus to a specific age group (18–25 years old), which is a group of patients who have not yet fulfilled specific cultural goals (e.g. education, family, employment). Thus, Andrew finalised his research question as "What is the impact of thalassaemia disease on 18–25-year-old patients' social life and identity?" This will help him keep the experiences as similar as possible. In other words, Andrew decides that his group should be as homogeneous as possible. He will establish some ground rules with his participants, such as being as talkative and elaborative as possible so as to generate good-quality data, and he will pose questions on what his participants think about other patient's experiences so that he has some "shadowed data".

Since the range of acceptable number of qualitative interviews varies, Andrew decides to conduct 10 interviews (Francis *et al.*, 2010). Andrew will then code all 10 interviews and develop his codebook, which will work as a guide for reaching data saturation. From the codes he will construct themes per interview. He will initially measure the number of themes in the first interview. He will then measure the shared themes in the second interview (also found in the first interview) and identify any new themes. He will compare the themes from the third interview and identify any new themes. Andrew will come to the conclusion that he has reached saturation when he stops finding new themes. When this happens, he will reorder the sequences of his interview multiple times and recheck for saturation in order to ensure that saturation has indeed been achieved within his dataset of 10 interviews. If saturation in not achieved within his initial dataset, Andrew will conduct more interviews. Achieving saturation will indicate that Andrew has enough data or that his data has reached enough depth for him to analyse (Constantinou *et al.*, 2017).

Recording, transcription, coding and analysis

For Andrew to have detailed data, he needs to record and transcribe his interviews. Recording interviews is very important because Andrew needs to listen to the material in order to transcribe it. Therefore, interviews should be held in quiet locations and the recorder should be placed close to the speaker so that his or her voice is heard loudly and clearly. Transcription is another important aspect of analysing qualitative interviews, and it can be very demanding and time consuming. There are a few things that Andrew must consider before he starts transcribing the interviews. First, researchers must decide on how accurate and detailed the transcription should be. They may choose to transcribe the interview using the exact words said, or they may choose to type up the interview in brief. Also, researchers may transcribe everything said by the informants, as well as describe the body language, tone of the voice, pauses and so forth. McLellan *et al.* (2003) explained that researchers may be faced with the need to decide whether to include pauses, incomplete sentences, grammatical errors and so on. The authors came up with what they called the "Qualitative Data Preparation and Transcription Protocol", which gives researchers specific guidelines in terms of what and how to transcribe. McLellan *et al.* emphasised that researchers should transcribe everything, including non-verbal clues (see also Green and Thorogood, 2009). As he is studying patients' experiences, Andrew decides that it is best to transcribe the interviews verbatim, and he takes descriptive notes of the non-verbal cues that he will be receiving from the patients.

When Andrew is done transcribing the interviews, he will need to proceed with a pivotal part of qualitative research, which is the coding of the data. What is coding and how can it be carried out effectively? Basit (2003: 143) maintained that analysing data is the "dynamic, intuitive and creative process of inducting reasoning" and that coding is a critical part of this process. Basit explained that codes are labels that represent specific sections of text. Labelling data based on their common meaning helps to organise the enormous amount of information researchers obtain from interviews and to identify possible links between labels. Basit cited Miles and Huberman (1994), who presented two main ways of coding. First, researchers may start coding inductively, based exclusively on what comes out from the data. This is the main baseline of grounded theory as outlined by Glasser and Strauss (1967). Second, researchers may start coding by using predetermined codes, which may have been derived from reviewing the relevant literature, then moving on with new codes derived directly from the data. These two ways of coding have also been presented by Hsieh and Shannon (2005) with regard to content analysis of texts.

The question remains here for Andrew, however, to explore and make the final decision. How is coding actually done? Weston *et al.* (2001: 384) explained their reasoning and the process of creating a coding system and codebook in order to investigate "how experienced professors use reflection to improve their teaching and the nature of their reflective process". Weston *et al.* explained that coding is not purely an objective task and that it may be influenced by other factors, such as the working environment, the number of people who work on coding and analysis, the theoretical basis (interpretivist or grounded theory), the nature of the study and the decision to use existing codes or theories. Weston *et al.* explained in detail how they created their own coding system and codebook. They initially selected a few transcripts from each research participant and came up with two general categories: monitoring and control. Then they read the transcripts from each participant and scripted the themes that emerged more than twice under each category to help define the boundaries around each category. They then created two codes under each category and read the scripts again. With further reading of the scripts, they generated more codes and sub-codes. Following this, they reviewed the scripts and refined existing codes and sub-codes and repeated the process again until new codes stopped emerging. Based on this coding, they came up with their codebook, which they used for presenting and interpreting the data. They went a step further in order to ensure validity. Through a dialectic process (constantly reviewing and refining codes at a committee level) and by receiving feedback from other colleagues at conferences and from participants, the authors ensured that the codes represented what they claimed they represented. Reliability was also a challenge for the authors, who managed to achieve this by making the coding consistent across coders. That is, coders were trained to make sure they interpreted the data in the same way, and a committee consisting of all six authors reviewed and refined the codes in a dialectic process. Finally, all the coders coded 10 per cent of the data from each participant in order to make sure that the coding was consistent. Though validity and reliability are not widely used in qualitative research, Welsh (2002) also highlighted their importance and that software for coding and analysing qualitative data contributes to consistency and coding accuracy.

The coding process and codebook that Weston *et al.* (2001) described relied on a deductive process, in the sense that they used existing codes to start with, but also on a "general inductive approach" (Thomas, 2006), which refers to the creation of new codes that arise directly from the data. This is similar to grounded theory in terms of the process of coding, but it differs from grounded theory in the sense that researchers who rely on grounded theory generate new theories during analysis, whereas a general inductive approach leads to the description and interpretation of data. Andrew decides to proceed with a general inductive approach but also to use a set of codes from the existing literature to start coding and then generating more codes from his own data. Thus, Andrew will need to report on his data based on what Weston *et al.* (2001) suggested about the description and presentation of results. This will happen through organising the presentation of data in sections which reflect codes and categories and by incorporating quotes from the actual data as representative examples of these codes. Including quotes from the actual data makes the presentation of data realistic. The interpretation of results is a different process and is done using existing research findings, theories and concepts.

Conclusion

Andrew reviewed the literature related to the social aspects of thalassaemia and qualitative research methodology before arriving at the decision to use in-depth interviews for understanding and reporting on the impact that thalassaemia has on the social life and identity of patients aged 18–25 years old. Through in-depth, semi-structured interviews and a structured plan for reaching data saturation and coding, Andrew is confident enough about achieving his research goals. Qualitative, in-depth interviews offer a few advantages to Andrew's study. More specifically, they allow Andrew to go into depth and understand the experience of thalassaemia in detail; they give participants the opportunity to narrate their experiences as they wish; and they provide answers to questions quantitative research cannot address, such as why what is happening is happening. Due to these advantages, qualitative interviews are very often combined with quantitative questionnaires in a mixed research methodology so that research can provide both an overall generalisable picture as well as in-depth understanding.

References

Basit TN (2003) Manual or electronic? The role of coding in qualitative data analysis. *Educational Research* 45(2): 143–154.

Bowen G (2008) Naturalistic inquiry and the saturation concept: A research note. *Qualitative Research* 8(1): 137–152.

Bowling A (2014) *Research Methods in Health: Investigating Health and Health Services* (4th ed.). Berkshire: McGraw-Hill.

Bryman A (2001) *Social Research Methods*. Oxford: Oxford University Press.

Caro JJ, Ward A, Green TC, Huybrechts K, Arana A, Wait S and Eleftheriou A (2002) Impact of thalassemia major on patients and their families. *Acta Haematologica* 107: 150–157.

Constantinou SC, Loizou C and Phellas NC (2014) Living with thalassaemia in Cyprus. In: *European Association of Social Anthropologists (EASA) 13th Biennial Conference Collaboration, Intimacy, Revolution*. Tallinn, Estonia, 31 July – 3 August 2014, p. 197. EASA.

Constantinou CS, Georgiou M and Pedikogianni M (2017) A comparative method for themes saturation (CoMeTS) in qualitative interviews. *Qualitative Research*. Epub ahead of print. DOI:10.1177/1468794116686650.

Georganda ET (1988) Thalassemia and the adolescent: An investigation of chronic illness, individuals, and systems. *Family Systems Medicine* 6(2): 150–161.

Gharaibeh H, Amarenh BH and Zamam SZ (2009) The psychological burden of patients with beta thalassemia major in Syria. *Pediatrics International* 51: 630–636.

Gollo G, Savioli G, Balocco M, Venturino C, Boeri E, Costantini M and Forni GL (2013) Changes in the quality of life of people with thalassemia major between 2001 and 2009. *Patient Preference and Adherence* 7: 231–236.

Guest G, Bunce A and Johnson L (2006) How many interviews are enough? An experiment with data saturation and variability. *Field Methods* 18(1): 59–82.

Hadzouli, A. (2012) *Thalassemic Lives* (in Greek). [Χατζούλη, Α. Θαλασσαιμικές Ζωές. Αθήνα: Εκδόσεις Πατάκη; 2012.]

Hsieh H and Shannon SE (2005) Three approaches to qualitative content analysis. *Qualitative Health Research* 15(9): 1277–1288.

Morse JM (2000) Determining sample size. *Qualitative Health Research* 10(1): 3–5.

Prasomsuk S, Jetsrisuparp A, Ratanasiri T and Ratanasiri A (2007) Lived experiences of mothers caring for children with thalassemia major in Thailand. *Journal for Specialists in Pediatric Nursing* 12(1): 13–23.

Roy T and Chatterjee SC (2007) The experiences of adolescents with thalassemia in west Bengal, India. *Qualitative Health Research* 17(1): 85–93.

Schutt RK (2004) *Investigating the Social World: The Process and Practice of Research*. London: Pine Forge Press.

Sherman M, Koch D, Giardina P, Hymowitz P, Siegel R and Shapiro T (1985) *Annals of the New York Academy of Sciences*, 328–336.

Silverman J, Kurtz S and Draper J (2013) *Skills for Communicating with Patients* (3rd ed.). Boca Raton, FL: CRC Press.

Thomas DR (2006) A general inductive approach for analyzing qualitative evaluation data. *American Journal of Evaluation* 27(2): 237–246.

Welsh E (2002) Dealing with data: Using NVivo in the qualitative data analysis process. *Forum: Qualitative Social Research* 3(2): 3–9.

Weston C, Gandell T, Beauchamp J, McAlpine L, Wiseman C and Beauchamp C (2001) Analysing interview data: The development and evolution of a coding system. *Qualitative Sociology* 24(3): 381–400.

Yalcon SS, Durmusoglu-Sendogdu M, Gumruk F, Unal S, Kargi E and Turgul B (2007) Evaluation of the children with β-Thalassemia in terms of their self-concept, behavioural, and parental attitudes. *Journal of Pediatric Hematology/Oncology* 29(8): 523–528.

4 Focus groups

Multiple sclerosis

Abstract

A young clinician and researcher, Dr Julie Anderson, would like to understand how young patients, 20 to 30 years old, cope with the psycho-social consequences of multiple sclerosis. She has interviewed two young women, aged 27 and 23, but feels that her participants are not expressing very much, given that they presented themselves as relatively healthy and happy with their lives and their future expectations. After conducting a third interview, she realises that her participants tend to compare themselves with her and they do not want to present themselves in a disadvantageous light. Therefore, Dr Anderson is reading through the literature to find other ways to understand her patients' experiences.

The experience of multiple sclerosis is the main focus of this chapter, which applies the qualitative method of focus groups to investigate the experiences of a specific age group of patients with this degenerative disease. The concept of focus groups is explained as being the ideal research method for this case, because it makes participants feel equal in a group of people with the same condition and allows them not only to share experiences but also to challenge each other.

Learning objectives:

- Explain the uses of focus groups.
- Describe the process of organising and running a focus group.
- Explain how data saturation is reached in focus groups.
- Describe the process of coding and analysing focus groups.

Scenario

A young clinician and researcher, Dr Julie Anderson, would like to understand the experiences of young patients, aged 20 to 30 years old, who live with multiple sclerosis. The experience of living with multiple sclerosis was the general framework that Julie wanted to explore. Her research question was "How do young patients, aged between 20 and 30 years old, cope with the psychosocial consequences of multiple sclerosis?" She interviewed two young ladies, aged 27 and 23, in order to pilot her interview questions and formulate an idea of how patients experience the disease. However, she felt that her participants were not providing her with very much information, as they presented themselves as relatively healthy and happy with their lives and their expectations for the future. Following the third interview, she realised that her participants tended to compare themselves with her and did not want to present themselves as disadvantaged in any way. Julie had read the literature before doing the pilot interviews and knew that having multiple sclerosis was a restricting experience. After conducting the pilot interviews, she initially thought that multiple sclerosis was not as restricting as she expected and that, perhaps, she was biased towards the disease and its consequences. If multiple sclerosis is not as constraining as is often thought, this should be documented in the literature. Therefore, Julie turns to the social sciences literature once more in order to check her participants' behaviour.

Multiple sclerosis as a psychosocial experience

Studies indicate that multiple sclerosis is a stressful disease, which may cause patients to feel uncertain about their future. Patients experience biographical disruption because the disease intervenes with many of their activities and hinders their quality of life as compared with individuals who do not suffer from the disease. Disruption is greater among people who are middle aged, as during this stage in life they are more financially active and have family commitments (Green *et al.*, 2007). An early study by Brooks and Matson (1982) focused on whether patients with multiple sclerosis adjusted to their condition effectively. Through the use of survey questionnaires, the authors found that patients with internal locus of control were more likely to adjust better, while those who came to terms with their condition were also more likely to adjust effectively. Furthermore, when patients had positive views of themselves, they experienced a better adjustment. Robinson (1990) analysed illness narratives of people with multiple sclerosis and revealed that his participants generally adopted positive approaches towards the consequences of the disease. A review of the literature by Antonak and Livneh (1995) indicated that people with multiple sclerosis went through severe psychosocial disruptions and changes in their lives. More specifically, people with multiple sclerosis reacted to the diagnosis of the condition in various ways. They experienced shock, anxiety, denial, depression, internal anger (blaming one's self), external hostility (being hostile towards others), acknowledgement (recognising the possible consequences) and adjustment. However, the problem with multiple sclerosis is not the diagnosis of the condition but its chronicity. That is, patients may experience chronic anxiety and depression, and they are more likely to experience depression compared with people with other conditions (Antonak and Livneh, 1995).

More recent research evidence shows that multiple sclerosis is a rather disruptive and distressing condition. More specifically, Amato *et al.* (2001) conducted a quantitative study to understand the impact of depression, fatigue and disability on 103 patients. The study showed that depression and fatigue had a negative impact on patients' quality of life. Interestingly, depression and fatigue had a greater impact than disability on patients' quality of life. Leon *et al.* (2002) wanted to know the association between cognitive and emotional functioning and health-related quality of life. Their quantitative study of 209 patients indicated that the more severe the condition, the greater the impact on patients' cognitive skills and emotions. It is worth noting that cognitive functioning improved among remitting patients. Along similar lines, Beiske *et al.* (2007) measured health-related quality of life of 345 patients from Norway, Sweden, Denmark and Finland. The authors found that disability, depression, fatigue and pain were the main factors negatively affecting patients' quality of life. Moreover, younger patients experienced greater social isolation as well as more fatigue and registered higher scores in the disability scale. The authors concluded that fatigue and reduced mobility had a negative impact on patients' sociality/sociability.

Kleiboer *et al.* (2007) aimed to investigate a more specialised topic by looking into the relationship between partners' beliefs and patients' mood. The authors recruited participants through convenient sampling by inviting patients to the Multiple Sclerosis Centre and Hospital in the Netherlands. Sixty-one people were eligible to participate in the study. The results revealed that patients experienced negative responses from their partners and, as a result, they were more likely to be stressed. Interestingly, younger and highly educated patients were more likely to present negative responses. The study also showed that negative responses and the resulting stress were ameliorated by the emotional support individuals received from their partners. This is because emotional support caused patients to feel less rejected and that their relationship was less likely to be in jeopardy. In other words, regardless of any negative responses, patients felt that they were still cared about by their partners when their partners provided emotional support at the same time.

Qualitative studies support the findings outlined above. Flensner *et al.* (2003: 710) interviewed patients with multiple sclerosis to understand how fatigue was experienced. They identified that patients experienced fatigue in many ways. More specifically, fatigue felt like "discharging a battery of energy". Gabriella, a patient, felt as if something had invaded her body and paralysed it. As a result, she did not trust that her body would support her wishes and behaviour, and thus started feeling uncertainty. Other patients said that they experienced fatigue all the time and that they had to plan their activities in order to manage them more effectively. This was because they needed to rest during the day in order to carry on. Therefore, they understood fatigue as "consuming and all-absorbing" (p. 711). Interestingly, for some patients, the body existed as an independent entity, which did not allow them to do the things they wanted. Patients were also emotionally affected because feelings of shame accrued due to the difficulty of being as productive at work as before. Apart from experiencing fatigue as a restriction, patients feared dependency, as they were anxious about the possibility of having to depend on others. However, patients were not holistically negative towards multiple sclerosis and experiencing fatigue. That is, some patients felt that they became stronger and thus found ways to live with their condition. To do so, they scheduled their daily lives as much as they could in order to accommodate this. Over time, patients made multiple sclerosis and any assistance they needed an integral part of their everyday lives.

Boeije *et al.* (2002: 882–885) interviewed 22 multiple sclerosis patients who lived at home to understand how they coped with the disease. They focused more specifically on "biographical work", which consisted of four parts. First, "contextualising" refers to making the condition part of one's biography. Second, "coming to terms" is the time when patients accept their condition. Third, patients "reconstitute [their] identity" by redefining their identity based on what they can do and thus arriving at a new wholeness. Fourth is "recasting biography", whereby patients find new contexts for their future biographies. Participants understood multiple sclerosis as "body failure" and they tried to position it in time by constructing a "time map" of the disease. They also viewed it as increasingly losing their independence. The authors presented four cases of biographical work, which showed that patients may have difficulties in recasting their biographies even when they accept multiple sclerosis and make the necessary changes in their lives in order to accommodate any resulting needs. Furthermore, some patients found it difficult to incorporate multiple sclerosis in their lives and to find new meaning in life. Green *et al.* (2007) conducted a quantitative study to measure a qualitative term: biographical disruption. The aim of the study was to measure the social, economic and emotional disruption among patients with multiple sclerosis. The study found that multiple sclerosis has a negative impact on employment, as patients were less likely to be employed than their healthy counterparts. Indeed, the greater the disability resulting from multiple sclerosis, the less likely patients were to be employed. Multiple sclerosis also disrupted marital relationships due to patients' increasing dependency on their partners and likely sexual dysfunction.

Discuss

- What could Julie learn from the relevant literature?
- Does the literature support the behaviour of her participants?
- If not, what should her next steps be?

Julie understands that multiple sclerosis is a psychosocial burden for patients and a restricting experience. Interestingly, Julie's participants do not seem to have experienced what the literature above indicated. Julie thinks of two possibilities: (1) her participants were in the minority who have not met with any serious consequences or (2) her participants were not as forthcoming in their interviews because they did not want to appear inferior to her. At this stage, Julie thinks that she now has two options: either she can carry on with more interviews or she can try a different research approach. Julie decides to explore other qualitative research methodologies and subsequently looks into the use of focus groups.

Definition and use of focus groups

A focus group is a group discussion of a particular topic (Wong, 2008). A number of people who share similar characteristics or experiences may be recruited to express and share their views in an interactive setting. The group may consist of 6 to 10 people, while the ideal number appears to be 8, as a small group does not yield much interaction, while a large group can potentially make discussion too complicated and difficult to manage. Norman (cited in McCrorie, 2010: 126) conducted an email survey to examine the size of problem-based learning (PBL) groups at medical schools around the world. Norman found that the most common PBL group size was eight. Though a focus group is not the same as a PBL group, they share some common features, such as focusing on a topic for discussion, reflecting on questions, managing group dynamics and the role of the facilitator.

There are a few advantages of using focus groups. First, focus groups may be used as grounds for other research methodologies. For example, researchers may organise one or two groups in order to gauge the situation and get ideas from participants with regard to a topic of interest (Wong, 2008). Thereafter, researchers may refine their research question, come up with questions to include in their interview guide, and formulate questions for the closed questionnaire they are constructing. Second, focus groups can be used as a supplementary research methodology to both qualitative and quantitative research methods. In other words, focus groups could contribute to a triangulation of research findings and make data more robust. Third, researchers may use focus groups as a stand-alone method for understanding phenomena that other methods cannot adequately explore. Unlike interviews, focus groups could, for example, explore the views of many people on a particular topic. Furthermore, Rabiee (2004) suggested that focus groups are useful for exploring sensitive topics, given that the group is homogeneous, as it is possible to create a pleasant and friendly environment for participants.

Julie's case falls into the third use of focus groups, because she is using them as an alternative to in-depth interviews. This is because she wants to gain an insightful and deeper perspective on her patients' experiences. On these grounds, Julie decides to use focus groups as a stand-alone methodology in order to answer her research question "How do young patients, aged between 20 and 30 years old, cope with the psychosocial consequences of multiple sclerosis?" Since her interviewees' experiences did not match the relevant literature with regard to the consequences of multiple sclerosis, Julie decided to change her research methodology and bring a number of patients with multiple sclerosis together to discuss their views and experiences. In such a group setting, young patients would feel that they were among peers and, therefore, more comfortable with expressing any negative experiences they might have had. Julie would like to make sure that the participants in each group do not know each other so that they may feel more comfortable with opening up and sharing intimate aspects of their lives. However, Julie has never run a focus group before and wonders how this should be done.

Discuss

- How should focus groups be organised?
- Should Julie organise focus groups based on what she is studying or should she follow the main guidelines? Justify your answer.

How a focus group can be organised and run

Tong *et al.* (2007) explained that before organising focus groups researchers should decide on the theoretical framework they would rely on for the conceptualisation and analysis of the data. More specifically, Julie could use grounded theory (construct theory out of data), ethnography (understand a small group or culture), phenomenology (understand the meaning of human behaviour), discourse analysis (focus on linguistics and use of language) or content analysis (understand the meaning of expressed words). Content analysis, as used by Tong *et al.* (2007), is similar to thematic analysis or the "general inductive approach" (Thomas, 2006) (see also Chapter 3). Julie is conducting a thematic analysis based on an inductive approach because she will be constructing codes or categories directly from her raw data. Julie now needs to think about how she will recruit her participants and organise the focus groups.

Recruiting participants for focus groups is a critical part of the process. In the event that Julie cannot find motivated participants, she may end up with a group that is not very dynamic and thus is less likely to provide her with important information for her study. Julie, therefore, considers locating her participants through either convenient sampling or the snowball method. To sample conveniently would require contacting patient groups, while snowballing would involve identifying a couple of patients to begin with and then asking them to suggest other potential participants. However, bearing in mind how her interviewees behaved when she tried to understand their experiences, Julie thinks that neither convenient nor snowball sampling is appropriate in her case, because she may end up with people who are not motivated to share their experiences or participants who know each other and thus may be less likely to express themselves freely.

Following the approach of other researchers, Julie thinks that it is best to recruit people by announcing her research in the press and the media and requesting that potential participants contact her. In the announcement she plans to include specific information about the inclusion criteria, such as that participants must be between 20 and 30 years old, male or female, must have been diagnosed with multiple sclerosis for at least 6 months and must be willing to express and share their views and experiences in a group setting. Julie plans to pay participants a small amount to cover their travelling expenses to the place where the focus groups will be held, and she decides to include this information in the announcement in order to make sure that she is not losing potential participants. Julie should make participants aware that they are expected to contribute to the discussion and that they may need to discuss some personal information that pertains to their condition. Rabiee (2004) maintained that participants should be selected on the basis of their suitability to the topic, as group dynamics are important for focus groups. Rabiee further argued that focus groups should be as homogeneous as possible so that other participants can relate to the expressed views. Some heterogeneity is fine, but researchers should monitor it carefully because it may create a threatening environment and discourage participants from continuing to contribute to the discussion. Though most scholars explain that it is better when participants do not know each other, Rabiee asserts that using pre-existing groups to explore sensitive topics might be better because participants can predict one another's stance.

When she has a good number of participants to form at least three groups, Julie can start running the focus groups and, at the same time, continue recruiting additional people to participate in more groups. The allocation of the participants to groups is critical. Julie does not want to mix them all up and have participants with very different experiences, because the group discussion may result in an individual talking to the researcher rather than an exchange of views between the participants. Therefore, Julie organises her groups according to two main categories: first, those who are younger and may still be in university; second, those who are employed and have families. In the second group, younger patients in their early twenties who are employed and have families may participate. There are a few advantages to organising her groups in this way. Her younger participants, who are university students, will be in a context where everybody else is a student and thus feel comfortable with discussing their experiences. If mixed with employed individuals with families, they might feel intimidated or feel like underachievers when comparing themselves with other patients who have managed to obtain a degree and/or have found work and started a family of their own. By organising her groups in this way, Julie will likely be able to moderate the discussion more effectively and in a more focused way. Furthermore, she will have a clearer indication of when to stop running focus groups once the data are saturated. This is discussed in more detail in the next section.

Julie reads other relevant studies and intends to observe focus groups in order to familiarise herself with the process of effectively running such groups. Julie knows that a group should consist of around eight participants. A moderator and an assistant moderator should be involved (Wong, 2008). The moderator or the interviewer initiates the discussion, poses questions to the group and makes sure that participation is as balanced as possible. In addition, Rabiee (2004) argued that the moderator should keep a diary to write down his or her general impressions of the discussion, non-verbal cues and his or her reflections on the moderation of the focus group discussion. The information from the diary could be substantial for refining the transcripts and the analysis of the raw data. To help her with this, Julie will have a semi-structured discussion guide. This will help her to explore specific questions that directly relate to her research question; however, she will leave enough room to add questions that are likely to arise during the discussion. However, unlike a semi-structured questionnaire in interviews, Julie should be mindful to have only a few questions on paper, for two main reasons. First, if she has many questions, the group discussion will be restricted to the questions. Second, a group discussion may result in coming up with many questions during the discussion. If Julie has many questions on her paper, she may omit important issues raised during the discussion, which she might never have considered before. Since a focus group moderator may strongly direct the discussion, Wong (2008) suggested piloting both the discussion guide and the moderator's style and direction before running the actual focus groups. It would be good if this pilot focus group was video-recorded or peer-reviewed so that the moderator could reflect on how the focus group ran. It might be necessary to implement revisions to both the style of moderation and the discussion guide before moderating the official groups that will be included in the study. An assistant moderator should focus more on the individual expressions and take notes on who said what and in what order. Also, the assistant moderator should take notes on the non-verbal communication. Without this information, transcription of focus groups would be difficult. In this way, the notes could then be compared with the transcripts and assist with filling in any gaps.

Another critical aspect of moderating a focus group is asking questions. The principles of asking questions are the same as those when conducting interviews. However, Julie may find herself in a dynamic environment, where many new issues arise from the conversation, which need immediate enquiry. To deal with such a busy environment, Julie needs to be alert and to pick up on the new issues that arise before the group moves on to the next issue. If Julie cannot interfere to ask a question, she could make a note and ask the question at a later stage during the discussion. Julie would need to be trained and know the existing literature on her topic well in order to be able to link the new issues with possible additional questions. Julie, like Andrew in Chapter 3, has the same problem to solve: "How many focus groups shall I run in order to have enough data to answer my research question?"

Discuss

- When should Julie stop running focus groups?
- Should she adopt the same strategies as used in interviews to reach data saturation?

Sampling and data saturation in focus groups

Though Julie can organise her groups reasonably and sensitively, she is not entirely certain as to when she should stop sampling. In qualitative studies, researchers stop sampling when they reach data saturation; that is, when no new themes or information can be derived from the data. What this means in practical terms has not been addressed adequately. Many researchers publish qualitative research noting that they stopped sampling when they stopped obtaining any new information or insight from the data (Bowen, 2008). However, this is not always acceptable to journal peer reviewers, and researchers are required to describe the exact practical processes involved in taking the decision to stop gathering more data. As discussed in Chapter 3 (Qualitative interviews), Bowen (2008) suggested that having the constructed themes in more than 70 per cent of interviews should be considered as having reached saturation, while Guest *et al.* (2006) conducted and coded a large number of interviews and then checked for data saturation in every six interviews. They coded 30 interviews and concluded that they reached saturation at the twelfth interview. Fancis *et al.* (2010) focused only on shared beliefs by at least two participants, and when they reached zero shared beliefs they applied the plus-three interviews criterion in order to achieve saturation. If there were no new shared beliefs after coding the three additional interviews, they concluded that saturation had been achieved. Constantinou *et al.* (2017) constructed a more holistic method (comparative method for themes saturation, CoMeTS), which included all themes, compared all interviews with each other and reordered the sequence of interviews before achieving saturation (see Chapter 3 for a more detailed presentation of these methods).

For focus groups, however, the 70 per cent threshold would not work adequately because group discussions can be very dynamic and may yield new, important information. Also, adopting Guest *et al.*'s approach may not be feasible, as organising, transcribing and analysing focus groups is more time-consuming than with interviews. Fancis *et al.*'s shared themes by at least two focus groups and the plus-three criterion cannot not work due to the small number of focus groups. Julie considers CoMeTS to be the most appropriate method for checking for saturation of themes in focus groups. That is, she will code the first focus group in each category (younger university students and employed with families), construct themes and measure the number of themes. Let us assume that Julie records 15 different themes. She will then code the second focus group and measure how many themes are the same as those in Group 1 and how many themes are new. Let us assume that Group 2 has 10 of the themes of Group 1 and 5 new themes. In the third group, there are 10 themes that are found in Groups 1 and 2 and two new themes. Julie could carry on like this until a group includes all the codes found in the previous groups and elicits no new codes. She could then run another focus group to double check that data saturation has been achieved. Group 4 has 12 themes and Group 5 has 11 themes found in the previous three groups and zero new themes. Table 4.1 shows Julie's strategy for reaching data saturation based on CoMeTS. Julie would then reorder the sequence of focus groups and check again for saturation in order to avoid the order-induced error and confirm that saturation has been achieved (Constantinou *et al.*, 2017: 13). Adopting this approach, Julie will need to work between running focus groups and coding, which may be challenging. However, she will make sure that she reaches saturation without having to run many focus groups.

Discuss

- Is the process of transcribing and coding of focus groups similar to that for interviews?
- What might make transcribing and coding of focus groups challenging?

Table 4.1 Data saturation

Focus groups	*Number of shared themes*	*Number of new themes per focus group*	*Total number of themes*
1	15	–	–
2	10	5	15
3	10	2	17
4	12	0	17
5	11	0	17

Transcription, coding and analysis of focus groups

In Chapter 3 (Qualitative interviews) we explained the process of transcription. That is, ideally, researchers should transcribe verbatim and keep notes on information that cannot really be transcribed, such as body language. To transcribe an interview verbatim is a demanding task and requires attention and time. To transcribe verbatim a focus group with around eight participants is a challenge that can be both time-consuming and tiresome. The complexity of interactions increases dramatically from one-to-one interview to a group discussion, while very large groups would make interactions too dense and complex to handle (Wong, 2008). It is advisable for either the moderator or the assistant moderator to transcribe immediately after the focus group ends, so that they can still remember the participants, their voices and what they generally said. Transcription could focus on two areas. First, Julie could measure the words that each participant uttered in the discussion. Julie could do this using software for coding and analysing qualitative data. This would give Julie an idea of how much each participant said and whether the discussion was balanced. Second, Julie could then code the discussion as she would code in-depth interviews, but she should be mindful with regard to the context of the question posed by the moderator or the context of the discussion. More specifically, coding should not be carried out in isolation; rather, it should always be done in the context of the discussion. This is because a participant would possibly not say something if this had not been triggered by other participants. To deal with this complicated task of coding, Julie or her assistant moderator could transcribe immediately after the end of the focus group or on the following day while the context of discussions was still fresh in the memory. While coding, Julie could add memos to the codes in order to contextualise them. Contextualisation of the codes would help Julie to find links between codes later on and to have a more complete picture of how her participants understand and cope with multiple sclerosis. Julie decides to use Weston *et al.*'s (2001) approach to coding qualitative data, as described in Chapter 3. Weston *et al.* prepared a detailed codebook which they used as a guide for coding all of their interviews. Similarly, Julie could create a codebook based on an inductive approach but also by using information from the existing literature. Her codes should then be accompanied by memos in order to help understand the origin of the relevant participants' expressions.

In principle, the analysis of focus groups does not differ from the analysis of in-depth interviews. However, coding and analysis of focus groups are more demanding and complicated, as Julie would have to present and interpret what a number of people told her individually while also explaining the dynamics observed in the groups and any conflicts or consensuses experienced at specific times during the group discussion. If Julie has a good codebook and detailed memos that contextualise the codes, the analysis will be much easier and more focused. Krueger and Casey (2015) explained that the analysis should be systematic and verifiable. This is to enable other researchers to verify the analysis and reduce subjectivity.

Krueger (1994) suggested a more specific approach to the analysis of focus groups. That is, researchers should have raw data that has been derived from focus group discussions. They should then come up with descriptive texts that represent units of information under similar categories and, finally, proceed with the interpretation of the data. Krueger went on to explain that interpretation should not be confined to separate codes but, rather, should reach out to encompass the relationship among codes. Therefore, interpretation should be organised into the following areas (Krueger, 1994): actual words used and their meaning, the context (circumstances under which comments were made), frequency and extensiveness of comments, intensity of comments (depth of expression), internal consistency (changing opinions), specificity of responses (what responses refer to) and big ideas (more general trends). Along similar lines, Wong (2008) posited that analysis should be organised into two main areas: first, the description of what has been said and second, the contextualisation of what has been said by identifying relationships between codes.

Kidd and Parshall (2000) looked at the literature on how to organise and run focus groups and found that there was not much information about the analysis of focus group discussions. One of the issues that researchers should deal with is that focus group participants very often formulate their opinion during the discussions. In other words, not only do they bring to the focus group their pre-existing views about the topic under investigation, but also they may change or come up with new ideas during the focus group. To deal with this challenge, Kidd and Parshall (2000: 399) suggested treating both the individual and the group as the "focus of analysis" and checking, through software, whether views were derived from controversies and arguments during the discussion. Also, qualitative analysis software can list all the views expressed by an individual and check for consistency across views or spot the exact moment the individual changed his or her point of view. In the case of a change, researchers should go back and put the change in the context of the discussion in order to understand what caused it. Another important aspect of the analysis is to understand whether a theme is indeed a group theme or whether it is something that came from a dominant participant. Software can help researchers list all the views under a theme and see whether the views expressed by different participants are similar enough to formulate a theme or whether most of the views actually came from one participant.

Validity and reliability are two important aspects that could make the results more robust. As with validity and reliability in in-depth interviews (see Chapter 3), researchers who use focus groups could deal with such challenges by making sure that the discussion guide is prepared by two people, the moderator is well trained, perhaps a second moderator could be present to make sure that the discussion guide is used as agreed, coding is done by two people separately, analysis is checked by a second researcher, and coding and analysis are systematic and continuous.

Discuss

- Now that she has decided not to use in-depth interviews, what are the advantages of focus groups in Julie's case?
- Are there any disadvantages that Julie should be aware of?

Conclusion

Going through the basic literature on the experience of multiple sclerosis and the use of focus groups in research, Julie decided that using in-depth interviews in order to understand how younger patients cope with multiple sclerosis was not a useful research methodology. This is because her participants tended to compare themselves with her and presented the condition as being not as restricting and stressful as Julie had expected. Therefore, knowing that focus groups are effective in exploring sensitive issues, she decided to recruit patients between 20 and 30 years old to participate in focus group discussions about what it means to live with multiple sclerosis and how individuals cope with it. By collaborating with an assistant moderator, she is transcribing verbatim, coding systematically, honing her moderation style, contextualising codes using software memos, keeping notes in her diary, and having her coding and analysis peer-reviewed or checked by another researcher.

Focus groups have some advantages over other research methodologies. First, researchers can generate a lot of data in a relatively short period of time. Second, focus groups can supplement other research methodologies, such as interviews and closed questionnaires, and can contribute to the triangulation of the data. Third, focus groups can be very useful in identifying areas for further exploration and topics that could be turned into questions to construct a new research tool for quantitative research. Fourth, they can stand alone and explore sensitive issues, such as views of people with HIV or, as in Julie's case, how younger patients cope with multiple sclerosis. However, focus groups also have various limitations. Aga and Macdonald (cited in Reed and Payton, 1997: 769) argued that focus groups are a "fast food" research methodology through which a researcher can obtain a lot of data in a short time but can end up with a superficial understanding of phenomena. This is why researchers should be careful when they opt to use focus groups as a stand-alone methodology for research. Moreover, results and conclusions can only be confined to the focus groups participants, data coding and analysis are time-consuming and demanding tasks, and moderation is highly demanding and requires training and reflection.

References

Amato MP, Ponziani G, Rossi F, Liedl CL, Stefanile C and Rossi L (2001) Quality of life in multiple sclerosis: The impact of depression, fatigue and disability. *Multiple Sclerosis* 7: 340–344.

Antonak RF and Livneh H (1995) Psychosocial adaptation to disability and its investigation among persons with multiple sclerosis. *Social Science & Medicine* 40(8): 1099–1108.

Benito-Leon J, Morales JM and Rivera-Navarro J (2002) Health-related quality of life and its relationship to cognitive and emotional functioning in multiple sclerosis. *European Journal of Neurology* 9: 497–502.

Beiske AG, Naess H, Aaarseth JH, Anderson O, Elovaara I, Farkkila M, Hansen HJ, Mellgren SI, Sandberg-Wollheim M, Sorensen PS and Myhr KM (2007) Health-related quality of life in secondary progressive multiple sclerosis. *Multiple Sclerosis* 13: 386–392.

Boeije HR, Duijnstee MSH, Grypdonck MHF and Pool A (2002) Encountering the downward phase: Biographical work in people with multiple sclerosis living at home. *Social Science & Medicine* 55: 881–893.

Bowen GA (2008) Naturalistic inquiry and the saturation concept: A research note. *Qualitative Research* 8(1): 137–152.

Bowling A. (2009) *Research Methods in Health: Investigating Health and Health Services*. London: Open University Press.

Brooks NA and Matson RR (1982) Social-psychological adjustment to multiple sclerosis: A longitudinal study. *Social Science & Medicine* 16: 2129–2135.

Constantinou CS, Georgiou M and Pedikogianni M (2017). A comparative method for themes saturation (CoMeTS) in qualitative interviews. *Qualitative Research*. Epub ahead of print. DOI:10.1177/1468794116686650.

Flensner G Ek A and Soderhamn O (2003) Lived experience of MS-related fatigue: A phenomenological interview study. *International Journal of Nursing Studies* 40: 707–717.

Francis JJ, Johnston M, Robertson C, Glidewell L, Entwistle V, Eccles MP and Grimshaw JM (2010) What is an adequate sample size? Operationalising data saturation for theory-based interview studies. *Psychology and Health* 25(10): 1229–1245.

Green G, Todd J and Pevalin D (2007) Biographical disruption associated with multiple sclerosis: Using propensity scoring to assess the impact. *Social Sciences & Medicine* 65: 524–535.

Guest G, Bunce A and Johnson L (2006) How many interviews are enough? An experiment with data saturation and variability. *Field Methods* 18(1): 59–82.

Kidd PS and Parshall MB (2000) Getting the focus and the group: Enhancing analytical rigor in focus group research. *Qualitative Health Research* 10(3): 293–308.

Kleiboer AM, Kuijer RG, Hox JJ, Jongen PJH, Frequin STFM and Bensing JM (2007) Daily negative interactions and mood among patients and partners with multiple sclerosis (MS): The moderating effects of emotional support. *Social Science & Medicine* 64, 389–400.

Krueger RA (1994) *Focus Groups: A Practical guide for Applied Research* (2nd ed.). California: SAGE.

Krueger RA and Casey MA (2015) *Focus Groups: A Practical Guide for Applied Research* (5th ed.). Los Angeles: SAGE.

McCrorie P (2010) Teaching and leading small groups. In: Swanwick T (ed.) *Understanding Medical Education: Evidence, Theory and Practice*. Oxford: Wiley-Blackwell, pp. 124–138.

Rabiee F (2004) Focus-group interview and data analysis. *Proceedings of the Nutrition Society* 63: 655–660.

Reed J and Roskell Payton V (1997) Focus groups: Issues of analysis and interpretation. *Journal of Advanced Nursing* 26: 765–771.

Robinson I (1990) Personal narratives, social careers and medical courses: Analysing life trajectories in autobiographies of people with multiple sclerosis. *Social Sciences & Medicine* 30(11): 1173–1186.

Tong A, Sainsbury P and Craig J (2007) Consolidated criteria for reporting qualitative research (COREQ): A 32-item checklist for interviews and focus groups. *International Journal for Quality in Health Care* 19(6): 349–357.

Wong LP (2008) Focus group discussion: A tool for health and medical research. *Singapore Medical Education* 49(3): 256–261.

5 Observation

Haemodialysis

Abstract

A PhD student and nurse, Alice Erickson, has just finished her analysis of quantitative and qualitative data from a study of patients who are undergoing dialysis. She found interesting data about the patients' quality of life and their understanding of dialysis based on measurements and in-depth interviews. However, Alice feels that there is a gap pertaining to how patients behave during haemodialysis. What words do they use to describe what is happening? How do patients interact with one another? Do they make jokes? What do they talk about during their dialysis?

These questions cannot be answered through closed questionnaires or in-depth interviews, as they require observation of behaviour. On this note, this chapter presents in brief the relevant literature related to living with end-stage kidney disease and uses observation as the main research method to record and understand the behaviour of patients in a specific context.

Learning objectives:

- Describe the main research findings from studies of the experience of haemodialysis.
- Explain what observation is and describe the steps to be employed to conduct observation effectively.
- Explain the advantages and disadvantages of observation.

Scenario

Alice Erickson, a PhD student and nurse, was interested in exploring how patients with end-stage kidney disease experience haemodialysis. She had worked at the Dialysis Department for many years and realised that haemodialysis is not merely a process of cleansing a patient's blood. Rather, it is an activity that has a far-reaching effect, affecting the individual as a social being, as well as the family and society. To further investigate the experience of haemodialysis, Alice formulated two main research questions. First, what was the impact of haemodialysis on the patient's quality of life? Second, how do patients understand haemodialysis, and what meanings do they ascribe to such a medical technology? To explore the first research question, Alice measured the quality of life of patients undergoing dialysis as compared with that of healthy people using closed and standardised questionnaires. For the second question, Alice conducted a number of in-depth interviews with patients with end-stage kidney disease.

Alice's study revealed very interesting results. She found that the quality of life of patients was worse than that of healthy people. In particular, she identified that quality of life worsened for younger patients who were between 25 and 45 years old. Alice attributed this finding to the observation that younger people had unfinished cultural goals (i.e. education, employment) or they still had many social obligations to fulfil (i.e. marriage, family). To support this quantitative finding, Alice conducted in-depth interviews with patients to understand more about the patients' experiences. Interestingly, she found a similar pattern. That is, though all patients presented dialysis as a difficult experience, younger patients used words with more negative connotations, such as torture, while a few older patients expressed positive attitudes towards haemodialysis in the sense that, under the circumstances, it was the means to survive. Alice was excited about being able to explore her research questions; however, she felt that there was more information and insight that she could not record merely through closed questions and interviews. Her many years as a nurse at the Dialysis Department had shown her that patients were not as negative as they sounded in the interviews, and they did not always seem to regard the haemodialysis room as a setting for suffering.

Discuss

- Why did Alice not manage to record everything she had experienced at the Dialysis Department through closed questionnaires and in-depth interviews?
- Could these two research methods be wrong or inadequate?
- What should Alice do next to understand why there is a discrepancy between her research findings and her experience as a nurse at the Dialysis Department?

Alice wants to do further research and she knows that other research methods might be able to help her fill in any gaps she thinks can be identified in her existing research findings. Therefore, before she decides what research method to employ, she first revisits the relevant literature to understand more about how patients experience chronic illness and haemodialysis.

The chronic illness experience and the experience of haemodialysis

Chronic illness is largely a contemporary phenomenon, resulting from increased life expectancy and the health problems that derive from ageing populations

(Higgs, 2008). As a result, people may find themselves with a chronic condition that may require them to make various lifestyle changes so as to accommodate their new experience – this is known in the literature as the "illness experience".

Pierret (2003) analysed the parameters of illness experience in the sociological literature. He explained that research on illness experience emerged in the 1960s and 1970s by working with Parson's concept of the sick role. Both quantitative and qualitative studies followed and focused on the subjectivity of a disease and the role of social structures. Pierret (2003: 8, 11, 14) went on to identify three main areas of concentration. First was the "subjectivity of illness experience". Here, research focused on how patients themselves understood their condition, the changes they had to make in their lives and how they narrated their experiences: terms such as stigma and shame, as well as how social differentials (i.e. age, gender, etc.) played a role in how patients experienced their health condition. In the second area, "strategies of coping: the illness experience in everyday life", patients found ways to deal with the condition and the changes to their lifestyles. The third area, "the illness experience and social structure", discussed the ways through which social contexts have an impact on how people experience their condition; for example, understanding the relationship between illness experience and socioeconomic status, ageing and modern society, technology, consumerism, globalisation and so forth.

An immediate consequence for chronic patients is what Bury (1982) has termed "biographical disruption", which refers to the disruption of one's social life and identity. Bury explained that such a disruption may occur in two ways. First, the patient may need to change their daily routine or lifestyle, such as their working hours, commuting, grocery shopping and so forth. Second, patients may experience a disruption of their biography, which refers to the contexts or structures through which people construct what defines them as social beings, such as being a parent, a husband, an employee and so on. Bury explained that patients do not merely go through a disruption of their lives but also, they respond to such a disruption. More specifically, they may try to make sense of the reasons behind the development of a disease; they may participate in a patient group or even adopt a new lifestyle to accommodate their concerns. Through their response, Bury argued, patients may renegotiate with their new experiences as an attempt to accept their new self. They do so through "coping", "strategy" and "style" (Bury 1991: 460–462). With coping, patients activate their cognitive template to compare their health condition with other more severe conditions in order to feel fortunate for not suffering more. Strategy refers to actions that patients take to deal with disruption, such as helping another patient who might be in greater need. Finally, patients may adopt a specific style to help themselves accept their condition more readily and lead a normal life. For example, chronic patients may adopt a heroic approach and present themselves as dealing with their condition in an outstanding way.

Biographical disruption as a concept is not without its weaknesses. Williams (2000) adopted a critical approach to the term and suggested a new direction in the way it should be used and researched. Williams argued that biographical disruption was useful for explaining the experiences of certain groups of patients but could not capture the variety and fluidity of experiences. More specifically, researchers should also take into account the type of the disease, the time it occurred, and experiences: a patient's prior experiences and background, and social circumstances. Williams concluded that "biographically related health experiences" should be explored as "a continuous theme in a changeable world" (Williams, 2000: 62). Following Williams' critical review of the term, several studies highlighted the fluidity of the term and the experiences of patients. For example, Levealathi *et al.* (2007), through their study of patients with cancer, came up with the term "biographical continuity", while Wilson (2007) described the experiences of their participants (mothers with HIV) as biographical reinforcement. Reeve *et al.* (2010) identified a biographical flow in their participants' narratives; however, Locock *et al.* (2009) found that patients with terminal motor neurone disease experienced a biographical abruption and, thus, aimed to redefine their lives to find new meaning in their remaining time. These studies of chronic illness stressed that biographical disruption was experienced; however, patients acted accordingly to carry on with their lives.

Patients with end-stage kidney disease who are undergoing dialysis treatment do not seem to be different in how they experience their disease. That is, they seem to experience both biographical disruption and biographical flow. To elaborate, White and Grenyer (1999) found that patients with end-stage kidney disease experienced feelings of anxiety and went through various lifestyle changes. Along similar lines, Aghakhani *et al.* (2014) highlighted that dialysis patients were afraid of dependency and viewed dialysis treatment as an unfriendly encounter. Interestingly, Curtin *et al.* (2002) interviewed 18 long-term dialysis patients and revealed that patients transformed their lives in a positive way. More specifically, they expressed optimistic views about their lives and the future and then came to terms with both the disease and its management. As a result, patients became very active in managing their own condition and lives.

Through in-depth interviews, Hargen *et al.* (2001) identified a mixture of positive and negative expressions towards end-stage kidney disease and dialysis treatment. Patients said that losing their freedom, being dependent on others and the disruption of their social and marital lives were what they experienced most strongly. On the other side of the spectrum, however, patients appeared to be optimistic and found ways to regain their autonomy. In a later study, Hargen *et al.* (2005) interviewed 41 patients between 29 and 86 years old, and found that patients experienced the disease as restricting and that they struggled to manage their condition and their life. Along similar lines, Gregory *et al.* (1998) showed that patients with end-stage kidney disease had difficulty dealing with dialysis but they also tried to be positive about living with a chronic disease. Cases *et al.*'s (2011) participants were even more positive. The participants in this study were long-term patients with end-stage kidney disease who were undergoing home dialysis. Patients had the opportunity to embed their treatment in their daily home schedule, and this resulted in giving them freedom and flexibility. In this case, patients restored their self-identity and became active in managing their condition and treatment.

Chronic patients, interestingly, do not merely express their feelings about their condition. Instead, they often select specific parts of their experiences to communicate their truth, or they employ what is called "illness narrative". According to Garro and Mattingly (2000: 12), a narrative "is a discursive presentation of events", which eventually reconstructs stories to the benefit of the narrator. Rosaldo (1986) asserted that narratives presented how things should be rather than how they actually are, while Frank (1995) stressed that a story is a tale whereas a narrative is a building block of several stories. A narrative, interestingly, consists of structure and content (Garro and Mattingly, 2000), which illuminates the institutional and socio-historical context in which it is developed. The structure of narratives refers to the building frameworks which house the content; this, for example, may take the form of a plot, while the content is made of blocks of meaning, which fill the structure to make the narrative a strong and impermeable coherent whole. Narratives do not necessarily represent the truth, but they represent a strategy of selectiveness, reordering, construction and coherence that reveals the ways in which a narrator makes sense of reality and chooses to present it (Kirmayer and Stern, 2004; Rapport, 2000). Kierans (2005) interviewed patients with end-stage kidney disease and found that patients constructed their narrative around the dimension of time, showing that dialysis slows time down. On these grounds, Kierans' (2005: 352) participants in Ireland were "future-oriented" because they hoped for a positive change in their life following transplantation. Along similar lines, Constantinou (2012: 26) found that patients with end-stage kidney disease in Cyprus envisioned their post-transplant self as a "proper human being" as they would not have to depend on the dialysis machine and would have the opportunity to fulfil social obligations without any restrictions. On this note, illness narratives have specific functions. They constitute selective parts of one's experiences and they aim to present a patient's experience in a very specific way. Patients do this as a way to legitimise their condition and what they are going through. For example, patients may place particular emphasis on the restricting nature of dialysis if they want to convince others that they are indeed suffering. Or they may stress that the condition itself helped them become better people if they aim at presenting it as a positive transforming experience.

Alice now has a guide to the discrepancy she found between her research findings and her own observations as a nurse. First, researchers should understand the contextualised illness experience, taking into account personal circumstances, prior health conditions, type of disease and so forth. Second, patients may experience one thing but present it to a researcher in a different way. This is because patients construct their own stories, which consist of selective experiences, in order to communicate subjective messages. Therefore, it could be the case that some of Alice's participants were generally satisfied with their treatment at the Dialysis Department and had accepted the fact that they had end-stage kidney disease, but they communicated a different story to her because they wanted to seem as though they were suffering and were in immediate need of a transplant. Given this insightful information from the literature, Alice decides to perform a systematic observation of patients at the Dialysis Department in order to address the research question "How do patients understand haemodialysis in relation to their body image and identity in a haemodialysis room?" However, Alice is concerned for two reasons. First, she is not sure how to conduct observation effectively. Second, she worries that her participants may change their behaviour because they will know that they are under observation.

Discuss

- How could observation be a challenging endeavour?
- Could participants indeed change their behaviour if they know that they are under study/being studied?

Observing the experience of haemodialysis

Observation is a technique of collecting research data through the senses, mainly through listening and observing in a natural environment (Bowling, 2002). The information that can derive from observation may be overwhelming, and this is what makes it a challenging endeavour. Without a plan and a systematic way of coding and analysing the data that derives from observation, researchers may find themselves at the brink of abandoning their study.

Through reading the relevant literature, Alice learned that observation can be structured or unstructured, overt, covert or participant (Bowling, 2002; Green and Thorogood, 2009). Structured observation refers to methods that are controlled and measured; for example, observe the number of people in a room, how the area is arranged, measure the number of interactions, number of smiles and so forth. Thus, structured observation can be quantitative. Unstructured observation is qualitative and aims at recording the meanings of social interactions in an environment. More specifically, a researcher could observe marriage rituals and the symbolic positioning of the groom, the bride and their parents. Whether structured or unstructured, observation can be overt (participants are aware of the presence of a researcher and that they are being observed), covert (participants are not aware that they are being observed) or participant (the researcher takes part in the participants' practices to understand those practices from the participants' perspective). Due to ethical issues, nowadays covert observation is rarely employed.

Whatever researchers decide to do, they must solve the issue of having access to the setting they want to study. However, access is not always offered but rather is gained, in the sense that researchers must try hard or follow a specific plan to make themselves welcome in the research setting. An effective way to achieve this is to make links with a mediator between the researchers and the community under study, starting with those who hold high positions in the management of the community (Bowling, 2002). Other ways could be for the researcher to spend some time with the potential research participants to socialise with them and explain to them the rationale behind the study. Furthermore, researchers should think of ways in which their research will be beneficial for both researchers and the community (Bowling, 2002). By doing so, they would create a relationship of trust between themselves and their research participants. Kuper (1988) described that some anthropologists had to change a research setting because they could not gain access to the community they wanted to study, either because they could not create an atmosphere of trust between themselves and those who would be observed or because they had difficulties in learning the language of the people they wanted to study. Interestingly, if a researcher aims at a covert observation, then access can be gained only if the researcher becomes a full member of the group he or she wants to investigate. For example, if a researcher wants to study the culture of a football fan club covertly, then he or she should become a full member of this fan club by adopting its acceptable dress code, symbols and way of thinking and by going to the arenas to support the football team.

In her studies, so far, Alice had learned about both qualitative and quantitative research methods and about research validity and reliability. However, how could Alice achieve validity and reliability through observation? Validity means that a research tool or a research method examines what it intends to study, whereas reliability refers to the consistency of a research method over time (Bryman, 2001). Anthropology, which relies on observation to understand human behaviour, has been criticised as non-scientific because it can demonstrate neither validity nor reliability. This is because observation, especially the unstructured type, is so uncontrolled and exclusively under the discretion of the researcher, who may introduce his or her biases into the study (so the actual focus is lost – no validity) and, thus, cannot produce similar results if the study is repeated in the future (no reliability). Given this, the study cannot be repeated by other researchers. Despite the arguments against them, anthropology and unstructured observation have their own logic, and validity and reliability can be achieved. Bowling (2002: 362–363) explained that "observer bias" can be minimised. Observer bias refers to the observer's interpretation of a happening which does not reflect the actual meaning of the happening. To deal with such a possibility, Bowling suggested that the use of two observers could be the solution. Hammersley and Atkinson (1995) maintained that through training of researchers in both observation and self-reflection, the impact of observation bias could be alleviated. Another dimension that the researcher needs to bear in mind is reliability, which can be achieved through ensuring the representativeness of observed data (Bowing, 2002). This can be done by observing enough during a representative time period.

Alice decides to proceed with a qualitative, unstructured, overt observation in the dialysis room. This is because she wants to understand more about the patients' social interactions and the meanings they ascribe to haemodialysis in the natural environment of a dialysis room. She cannot employ participant observation because doing so would require her to lie on a hospital bed and have her blood cleansed through the dialysis machine. As a result, she can only observe overtly. However, she is concerned with two things. First, knowing that they are observed, her participants may change their behaviour. For example, they may express highly positive attitudes to keep the nurses happy or they may be extremely negative in an attempt to bring about changes to the way the dialysis room is managed. Alice's concern reflects the Hawthorne Effect, which refers to the impact overt observation has on participants' behaviour (Bryman, 2001). Interestingly, participants may change their behaviour at the initial stages of observation; however, as time passes, they may get used to the researcher's presence and behave naturally. Second, Alice is not sure whether she should conduct the observation as a nurse (wearing the white coat) or as a researcher. Amit (2000) asserted that researchers should not interfere with the routine of the natural social environment they are observing. On this note, Alice thinks that it is better to perform the study while working as a nurse in the dialysis room. This is a challenging task, because Alice must find a way to act as a nurse so that she does not disrupt the flow of the dialysis procedures, while at the same time keeping herself away from her duties to observe more objectively. In anthropology, this has been called "being at home and away" at the same time (Caputo, 2000: 19), and anthropologists learn how to do this through experience and through reading several observational studies to learn how other researchers have managed to take on this dual role. Thus, Alice's plan is to observe overtly as a nurse and allow herself more time so that patients get used to her presence as both a nurse and a researcher.

Discuss

- Could Alice incorporate other techniques of collecting data during observation? Why?
- What other techniques might be the most appropriate?

Mere observation of human behaviour without using any other techniques at the same time could possibly leave Alice with unanswered questions at the end of her study (Hammersley and Atkinson, 1995). An effective technique to use during observation would be asking questions. This does not mean that Alice is performing in-depth interviews at the same time, but that she formulates questions that could help her clarify what she might not be able to understand through observation. Having prior experience with in-depth interviews, Alice would avoid leading questions or questions that ask multiple things at a time and would ask simple and specific questions. She decides not to interrupt the observed scene; instead, she will take notes and pose a question whenever circumstances permit, for example, when patients do not seem to interact with one another. Based on her knowledge of the functions of illness narratives, Alice thinks that it is best not to wait long after the observed scene before asking her questions so that the patients do not have the opportunity to reconstruct their interpretations. For example, if a patient says to another patient that the haemodialysis machine is "like a friend", Alice should ask a relevant question to clarify what the patient means as soon as the interaction between the two ends or as soon as she can (if she must focus on another interactive scene). As she narrows the gap between the observed scene and her questions, the responses she receives are likely to link directly to what she observed rather than to what patients remembered or would like to present. Moreover, questioning during observation is not the same as questioning during in-depth interviews. With in-depth interviews, questions are usually predetermined by the researcher, who leaves some flexibility to add questions should this be necessary. However, questions asked during observation are not predetermined but rather, are born of data. They are an integral part of observation – the researcher needs to be well trained to identify them and ensure that they are answered. Given this, it would make no sense to use predetermined closed or open-ended questions in an observed setting.

Coding and analysing observed data

Alice finds out that to code, she should record in detail and put on paper what has been observed (Green and Thorogood, 2009). However, how is she going to record so much detail when she should be paying attention to what she needs to observe? She could visually record what is happening in the dialysis room and then transcribe and code the content. This would secure detailed and precise data but would be very time consuming, because she would have to record many hours of social interactions over the course of several days. It would also elicit more ethical issues to handle, such as obtaining additional consent from all the people involved. Alice learns that anthropologists take notes during their observations and that they reorganise their notes at systematic intervals or following a few days of observation. Doing so offers advantages in managing the data. That is, researchers remember what has already been observed and so they can refocus their observation should they encounter areas that need more attention.

Alice decides to start taking notes during dialysis and refine her notes at the end of each day. At this point, she wonders when she should stop collecting data. Early anthropologists considered that the period of observation should be large enough to help the researcher understand in detail and in full the society of the phenomenon they were studying. Usually a period of two years was understood as good enough for this purpose (Kuper, 1988). However, early anthropologists studied small societies as total collectivities or focused on larger issues or social institutions, such as religion, family, initiation rituals and so forth. Alice, by contrast, is focusing on a specific group of patients who are under a specific form of treatment in a very specific environment. As a result, she should not need two years of observation. To select a cut-off time, Alice decided to carry on with observation until saturation of themes is achieved (Green and Thorogood, 2009) – this is usually used to decide where to stop in-depth interviews (see Chapter 3 for more information about the importance of saturation and the published methodologies for achieving it).

In Chapter 4, Dr Julie Anderson decided to adopt the CoMeTS method (Constantinou *et al.*, 2017: 13). Since organising and analysing focus groups is a demanding task, Julie decided to identify all the themes from the first focus group and then check how many of the existing and new themes were found in the following focus groups until no new themes could be generated. CoMeTS can also be used in Alice's case of observing the haemodialysis room. That is, Alice could take each observation day as a separate data item. She could stop observing at the end of a month (when 30 days are completed), have a break from observation, accumulate all her notes, code each day separately and construct themes. Alice could then code Day 1 and record all themes identified. For Day 2, Alice should try to identify any themes from Day 1 and record any new themes. She could then carry on until all themes from the previous days are found and no new themes are generated. She could then reorder the sequences of coded days and check again for saturation so as to avoid the order-induced error (Constantinou *et al.*,

2017: 13). On the grounds of this strategy for reaching saturation, Alice thought that observation would take two to three months. However, it may possibly take much longer for her to achieve saturation because of the variety of patients' backgrounds and experiences – age, ethnicity, gender, occupation and so on – and the various environments, such as different shifts, times of the year (e.g. summer, Christmas) and so forth.

Discuss

- How much information would Alice end up with?
- How should Alice handle the information she has?

Taking notes for months could give Alice an enormous amount of information, which would be meaningless if it remained as notes. Alice, however, is proactive enough to construct a template for coding before she starts the observation. Her aim is not to come up with new concepts or theories, which would refer to the adoption of grounded theory for analysis (Green and Thorogood, 2009), but rather, to understand as much as she can. Therefore, Alice once again reads the literature on illness experience and the experience of haemodialysis and makes a list of themes, such as disruption, identity, stigma, perceptions of the body and so forth, which she uses as general codes or umbrellas for her data. She should also leave room for more codes, which would be unique to her study. At the end of each day, she intends to type large portions of her notes under each predetermined or new code. After a while, she will be able to decide more readily whether the saturation of themes is about to be achieved, and she will have her data in two forms: first, the notes, which will be content specific; second, the coded data, which will specify the day and context they were taken from. Alice could then easily cross-match the coded data with her notes if she needs more information about the context in which the data were observed.

Discuss

- Is having the data organised and coded enough for understanding the phenomenon under study?
- What should Alice's next steps be?

What Alice should do next is to present the data in a more academic form and proceed with its interpretation and discussion. What does presenting observed data mean? Presenting observed data does not differ in principle from presenting data from qualitative interviews. That is, the data needs to be presented under topics, which could be the codes themselves or could reflect the codes. For example, under the topic "perceptions of the human body", Alice could include her participants' references to the ways they understand their body while connected to the dialysis machine. However, assigning large portions of participants' words to a topic is not a proper way of presenting observed data. Thus, Alice reads all the relevant words and constructs a text that will represent all these words, like finding the average from an array of numbers. In other words, what are the common themes that derive from all the words that relate to the perception of the human body? Common themes refer not only to similarities across words but also to differences, in the sense that different approaches adopted by participants constitute a common feature in their perceptions. To support her representative text, Alice could include a few extracts from the observed data. Like processing individual numbers, Alice is processing individual words and translating them into a description of a collective word or behaviour that represents the whole group under study.

Discuss

- What should the next steps be for Alice?
- How would the presented data make sense scientifically?

After Alice finishes the presentation of the observed data, she will need to interpret and discuss her data. Interpretation and discussion are where Alice can make sense of her observed data scientifically. Interpretation and discussion are not one and the same. Interpretation refers to understanding data in light of existing research findings and theory. For example, Alice could use Bury's concept of "coping" to explain that patients who are undergoing dialysis may activate their cognitive mechanisms to compare themselves with patients with more serious diseases in order to empower their sense of self. Discussion refers to a comparative framework in which Alice would compare and contrast her findings with those from other studies. Such discussion is helpful because Alice can identify similarities with other studies and make sense of any differences. By exploring the differences between her study and other studies, Alice could outline the reasons behind such discrepancies, which usually have to do with the different theoretical frameworks and research methods adopted, as well as the cultural factors at play across the various studies. A research study usually ends with a conclusion, which can be as important as the other parts. The conclusion is more than a summary of what the study has already reported. In the conclusion, Alice could identify issues that go beyond her study and areas for further research or ideas for the development of new theories and concepts. In other words, her conclusion could summarise what she studied and identified but also prepare the ground for what should follow.

Discuss

- What are the advantages of observation in Alice's case?
- Are there any disadvantages that Alice should be aware of?

Conclusion

Based on her experience in studying haemodialysis, Alice concludes that she cannot use whatever research method she likes to examine what she wants to study. Different research methods are more suitable in different contexts and for answering specific research questions. Her research question, "How do patients understand haemodialysis in relation to their body image and identity in a haemodialysis room?", cannot be adequately answered through closed questionnaires or in-depth interviews because it requires observing their behaviour and narratives in a natural environment (in this case, the haemodialysis room). Therefore, observation is the most suitable method to employ in this case. After using observation, in-depth interviews and closed questionnaires, Alice understands that observation has some advantages and disadvantages in this specific case. On the positive side, observation studies human behaviour in a natural environment as it is happening, explores processes in depth and uncovers the complexities, and the explanations derived are closer to the actual behaviours. On the negative side, observation is time consuming, requires a great deal of training and results in a large amount of information, and the explanations are specific only to the specific natural environment that is being observed.

References

Aghakhani N, Sharif F, Molazem Z and Habibzadeh H (2014) Content analysis and hemodialysis patients, family experience and perceived social support. *Iranian Red Crescent Medical Journal* 16(3): e13748.

Amit V (2000) Introduction: Constructing the field. In: Amit V (ed.) *Constructing the Field: Ethnographic Fieldwork in the Contemporary World*. New York: Routledge, pp. 1–18.

Bowling A (2002) *Research Methods in Health: Investigating Health and Health Services* (2nd ed.). London: Open University Press.

Bryman A (2001) *Social Research Methods*. Oxford: Oxford University Press.

Bury M (1982) Chronic illness as biographical disruption. *Sociology of Health & Illness* 4(2): 167–182.

Bury M (1991) The sociology of chronic illness: A review of research and prospects. *Sociology of Health & Illness* 13(4): 451–468.

Caputo V (2000) At "home" and "away": Reconfiguring the field for late twentieth-century anthropology. In: Amit V (ed.) *Constructing the Field: Ethnographic Fieldwork in the Contemporary World*. New York: Routledge, pp. 19–31.

Cases A, Dempster M, Davies M and Gamble G (2011) The experience of individuals with renal failure participating in home haemodialysis: An interpretive phenomenological analysis. *Journal of Health Psychology* 16(6): 884–894.

Constantinou CS, Georgiou M and Pedikogianni M (2017). A comparative method for themes saturation (CoMeTS) in qualitative interviews. *Qualitative Research*. Epub ahead of print. DOI:10.1177/1468794116686650.

Constantinou CS (2012) "Now I am a proper human being": Kidney transplantation in Cyprus. *Medical Anthropology*, 31(1): 29–43.

Curtin RB, Mapes D, Pertillo M and Oberley E (2002) Long-term dialysis survivors: A transformational experience. *Qualitative Health Research* 12(5): 609–624.

Frank A (1995) *The Wounded Storyteller: Body, Illness, and Ethics*. Chicago: Chicago University Press.

Garro LC and Mattingly C (2000) Narrative as construct and construction. In: Mattingly C and Garro LC (eds) *Narrative and the Cultural Construction of Illness and Healing*. Berkeley, CA: University of California Press, pp. 1–49.

Green J and Thorogood N (2009) *Qualitative Methods for Health Research* (2nd ed.). Los Angeles: SAGE.

Hammersley M and Atkinson P (1995) *Ethnography*. London: Routledge.

Hargen B, Petterson I, Severinsson E, Lurzen K and Clyne N (2001) The haemodialysis machine as a lifeline: Experiences of suffering from end-stage renal disease. *Journal of Advanced Nursing* 34(2): 196–202.

Hargen B, Petterson I, Severinsson E, Lurzen K and Clyne N (2005) Maintenance haemodialysis: Patients' experiences of their life situation. *Journal of Clinical Nursing* 14: 294–300.

Higgs P (2008) Later life, health and society. In: Scambler G (ed.) *Sociology as Applied to Medicine* (6th ed.). London: Elsevier, pp. 176–192.

Kierans C (2005) Narrating kidney disease: The significance of sensation and time in the emplotment of patient experience. *Culture, Medicine and Psychiatry* 29: 341–359.

Kirmayer LJ and Stern L (2004) Knowledge structures in illness narratives: Development and reliability of a coding scheme. *Transcultural Psychiatry* 41(1): 130–142.

Kuper A (1983) Anthropology and Anthropologists: The Modern British School. London: Routledge & Kegan Paul.

Levealathi H, Tishelman C and Ohlen J (2007) Framing the onset of lung cancer biographically: Narratives of continuity and disruption. *Psycho-Oncology* 16: 466–473.

Locock L, Ziebland S and Dumelow C (2009) Biographical disruption. Abruption and repair in the context of motor neurone disease. *Sociology of Health & Illness* 31(7): 1043–1058.

Pierret J (2003) The illness experience: State of knowledge and perspectives for research. *Sociology of Health & Illness* 25: 4–22.

Rapport N (2000) The narrative as fieldwork technique: Processual ethnography for a world in motion. In: Amit V (ed.) *Ethnographic Fieldwork in the Contemporary World*. London: Routledge, pp. 71–95.

Reeve J, Lloyd-Williams M, Payne S and Dowrick C (2010) Revisiting biographical disruption: Exploring individual embodied illness experience in people with terminal cancer. *Health* 14(2): 178–195.

White Y and Grenyer B (1999) The biopsychosocial impact of end-stage renal disease: The experience of dialysis patients and their partners. *Journal of Advanced Nursing* 30(6): 1312–1320.

Williams SJ (2000) Chronic illness as biographical disruption or biographical disruption as chronic illness? Reflections on a core concept. *Sociology of Health & Illness* 22(1): 40–67.

Wilson S (2007) "When you have children, you're obliged to live": Motherhood, chronic illness and biographical disruption. *Sociology of Health & Illness* 29(4): 610–626.

6 Longitudinal study

Heart disease

Abstract

John Bennett believes that the residents of the large, outer-city community where he lives are more vulnerable to heart diseases than people elsewhere and he argues that the number of residents who die from heart problems in this area has escalated in the last few years. Mr Bennett is interested in conducting a study to test his hypothesis.

This chapter provides a review of the sociological literature with regard to the social factors that contribute to the development of cardiovascular conditions and applies the main principles of longitudinal study in order to test the hypothesis that the residents in a specific urban community are more vulnerable to heart conditions.

Learning objectives:

- Review the sociological literature with regard to the social factors that contribute to the development of cardiovascular conditions.
- Explain how a longitudinal study design is applied and the different types of longitudinal study design.
- Identify the advantages and disadvantages of applying a longitudinal study design.

Scenario

John Bennett believes that the residents of the large, outer-city community where he lives are more vulnerable to heart diseases than people elsewhere and he argues that the number of residents who die from heart problems in this area has escalated in the last few years. John is interested in conducting a study to test his hypothesis. His initial research question was to find out whether cardiovascular disease (CVD) was more prevalent in a specific area. However, John is concerned about the possibility of leaving out important information, such as the impact of time and changes in people's social circumstances and habits. For example, if John does not find any differences between two geographical areas or two groups, this does not mean that there are no real differences, because his findings would only represent a snapshot of a specific point in time. Before John finalises his topic and research question, he would like to review the literature on the social aspects of CVD.

Social factors and the development of cardiovascular conditions

CVD relates to a group of severe heart conditions that include coronary heart disease, cerebrovascular disease, peripheral arterial disease, rheumatic heart disease, congenital heart disease and deep vein thrombosis, as well as pulmonary embolism (World Health Organization, 2015). Among high-income countries, CVD is considered to be responsible for 25 per cent of deaths (Levenson *et al.* 2002, cited in Kreatsoulas and Anand, 2010), whereas by the year 2030, it is estimated that CVD will be responsible for over 11 million deaths worldwide (Lopez *et al.*, 2006, cited in Kreatsoulas and Anand, 2010). In addition, low- and middle-income countries represent over three-quarters of CVD deaths (World Health Organization, 2015).

Several psychosocial factors, such as low socioeconomic status, social isolation, lack of social support, stress at work and in family life, depression, anxiety, hostility, anger and type D personality have been found to contribute to the development of cardiovascular conditions (Perk *et al.* 2012). According to a review conducted by Albus (2010), both genders with low socioeconomic status (e.g. low education, low income, low-status job, living in a poor residential area, etc.) have a coronary heart disease mortality risk (Leino *et al.*, 2000, cited in Albus, 2010). In addition, stress at work, especially in men, has been found to predict the onset of CVD (De vogli *et al.*, 2007; Eller *et al.*, 2009, cited in Albus, 2010), whereas in women stress attributed to family life is found to increase the risk of cardiovascular heart disease (Eaker *et al.* 2007, cited in Albus, 2010).

Several systematic reviews substantiate that social isolation and low social support are risk factors for developing CVD. The same applies to depression; both systematic reviews and meta-analyses reveal that clinical depression and depressive symptoms predict the incidence of CVD (Wulsin *et al.* 2003, cited in Albus, 2010) and worsen its prognosis (Barth *et al.* 2004; Van Melle *et al.* 2004, cited in Albus, 2010). Regarding the link between anxiety disorders and CVD, epidemiological studies (Chen *et al.* 2009; Smoller *et al.* 2007, cited in Albus, 2010) validate a connection between panic attacks and CVD (hazard ratio 1.7–4.2) (Chen *et al.* 2009; Smoller *et al.* 2007, cited in Albus, 2010). Additionally, personality traits such as hostility and anger are related to the onset of CVD incidences in healthy and cardiovascular heart disease populations (Chida and Steptoe, 2009, cited in Albus, 2010).

Furthermore, a prospective cardiovascular population study conducted in Copenhagen between 1976 and 2013, which aimed, among other things, to compare traditional and psychosocial risk factors and to rank them by importance for incidence of CVD in a random sample of 19,329 white men and women aged 20–39 years, revealed 1731 non-fatal and fatal coronary events. In relation to gender, men ranked highest in vital exhaustion and systolic blood pressure, whereas women ranked highest in smoking, followed by vital exhaustion (Schnohr *et al.*, 2015).

Importantly, a longitudinal study conducted in Dallas (Powell-Willey *et al.*, 2015), which aimed at exploring the relationship between moving to more socio-economically deprived neighbourhoods and weight gain as a cardiovascular risk factor, revealed a relationship between moving to a neighbourhood of higher socio-economic deprivation and increased weight gain in the Dallas Heart Study (DHS) cohort, which further suggested that cumulative duration of exposure to neighbourhood deprivation has an impact on the potential for obesity and obesity-related cardiovascular morbidity.

All these social factors, which are related to CVD, pertain to the issue of social inequalities in health. The Black Report in the 1980s is one of the early studies on health inequalities (Townsend and Davidson, 1990). For this study, the British population was organised into social classes based on people's occupation. There were six classes: Class I: professional, class II: intermediate, class IIIN: skilled non-manual, class IIIM: skilled manual, class IV: partly skilled, and class V: unskilled. The results showed that people from classes IV and V had higher rates of morbidity and mortality. Later studies, which used the same classification, highlighted similar results. Furthermore, people from classes IV and V were more likely to experience heart disease, lung cancer and respiratory disease (Bartley and Blane, 2008). Taylor and Field (2007) presented data to show that people in managerial positions were more likely to report good health, while those who worked full-time reported better health than those who worked part-time. An interesting question to consider is why these differences are observed between the social classes. Various approaches/models have been developed in order to answer this question: the materialist, the behavioural, the life course and the psychosocial.

The materialist approach relates to people's access to material resources, such as housing, work, healthcare and so forth. The behavioural model relates more to people's behaviour, which could potentially include risk factors for diseases. More specifically, behaviours such as smoking, alcohol consumption, drug abuse, unhealthy diet and lack of physical exercise are associated with health conditions such as cardiovascular and respiratory disease. Studies show that working-class people lack enough knowledge about the dangers connected to such behaviours (Layte and Whelan, 2009) and they are more likely to adopt a fatalistic view of life. That is, they tend to believe that their fate is predetermined and that there is little they can do to change it. Furthermore, Feinstein (1993) found that people from working-class backgrounds were less likely to utilise healthcare services, which could result in late diagnosis of conditions and poor prognosis.

The life course model focuses on the impact of time and experiences on people's health. Van de Mheen *et al.* (1998) explained that socioeconomic background in childhood is associated with socioeconomic background in adulthood. Also, health conditions in childhood tend to continue in adulthood and disadvantage adult patients. Van de Mheen's (1998) longitudinal study in the Netherlands showed that lower socioeconomic status in childhood is related to health inequalities in adulthood. The psychosocial model aimed to explain the psychosocial impact of lower socioeconomic status. Studies showed that working-class people are more likely to experience stress and are less likely to have good self-efficacy. Apart from these models, which are supported by research, there is another, rather controversial approach that relates to social selection (Roger and Pilgrim, 2010). Based on this approach, people who are more biologically vulnerable to getting sick tend to come from a lower socioeconomic background.

This information from the literature is very important, as it can help John refine his research question and formulate his hypotheses more clearly. Initially, when John thought that there were more incidents of CVD in the area in which he resides, he thought that this was due to environmental factors or genetics. However, this puzzled him, as the population has the same ethnic background as the population in other surrounding areas that do not show such high incidences. Thus, the reason for the higher incidences might be socially based; however, this needs to be explored carefully.

John now has a clearer research question: Does CVD develop more in a specific geographical area? Furthermore, John is interested in understanding the impact of specific social factors and formulates the following additional hypotheses: Low socioeconomic status may be associated with increased diagnosis of CVD; smoking and alcohol may be associated with increased diagnosis of CVD; unhealthy eating may be associated with increased diagnosis of CVD; and low health literacy may be associated with increased diagnosis of CVD. However, John is concerned that if he collects data at one point in time, he may miss important information about the impact of changes in people's lives and behaviour. Therefore, John considers taking into account the factor of time in order to assess the impact of various social characteristics on the onset of CVD. On this note, a longitudinal study design might be more appropriate for John's research questions/hypotheses because he can then understand how changes in his participants' socioeconomic status may have influenced the development and progress of heart disease or how changes in eating and smoking habits can influence his participants' heart health.

What is a longitudinal study design?

A longitudinal study design is a type of research design that serves best for measuring the extent of change in a phenomenon, situation, problem or attitude. Such a study design may be used to examine, for example, the change occurring over long periods of time in relation to a certain disease. In health sciences, it is used to discover predictors of certain diseases and usually includes tests or assessments, whereas in social sciences, it is used to explore significant life events throughout the lifespan. Longitudinal studies can collect data from households or families, organisations or larger social units, such as nations. Data collection is undertaken at regular intervals, over a long period of time. However, intervals are not predetermined; thus, their length varies from study to study (from weeks to years) and depends on the subject matter, context and issues addressed (Hakim, 1987).

The information gathered is always the same, but it is not gathered from the same participants (Kumar, 2005) and it could be quantitative or qualitative in nature (Alasuutari *et al.*, 2008).

National or large-scale studies are intended to provide data that is representative on a national basis for the type of group studied and can provide incidence or prevalence rates for a given behaviour, attitude or event, as well as information for the detailed analysis of its causes and consequences. National studies rely on a combination of three methods: interview surveys of sample members, data extracted from administrative records, and surveys of informants. A distinction is also made regarding the methods used in studies concerning children (data extracted from administrative records and survey of informants), whereas the methods used in studies concerning adults employ interview surveys of sample members and data extracted from administrative records. On the other hand, small-scale longitudinal studies are viewed as case studies and can employ a variety of data collection techniques. Overall, longitudinal studies provide information on gross changes at the micro-level or non-causal processes. A longitudinal study can therefore answer questions about causes and consequences and, thus, provide a basis for substantiated explanatory theory (Hakim, 1987).

Different types of longitudinal study designs

In order for John to decide on the type of longitudinal study, he has to delve more deeply into the literature. There are distinct kinds of longitudinal study designs, such as panel study, cohort study, and prospective, retrospective and retrospective-prospective study design (Bryman and Teevan, 2005). A panel study includes random data collection from households or schools, whilst a cohort study involves a homogeneous sample, either the entire cohort or a nationally representative sample that will be followed up over a period of time. A cohort is a group of people who have the same lived experience or characteristic (e.g. same date of birth or marriage, year of entry to an institution, etc.) (Hakim, 1987). Literature also identifies age cohorts (e.g. people born in the 1920s or people born in a single year or during one week of a single year). Panel studies are conducted over either short- or long-term intervals. The main difference between panel and cohort studies is that the former are concerned with all ages, which are constantly measured across the age range, as well as throughout the life course (Bryman and Teevan, 2005).

Additionally, at times, panel studies' contextual data (e.g. family income) have been analysed to study patterns of

- Unemployment, and to compare cross-sectional and longitudinal pictures on the distribution of unemployment (Hill and Concoran, 1979, cited in Hakim, 1987), fertility (Hofferth, 1983, cited in Hakim, 1987)
- Sex and race differentials in labour supply and earnings (Lloyd and Niemi, 1979; Parcell and Mueller, 1983, cited in Hakim, 1987)
- The work disincentive effects of unemployment insurance benefits (Capen *et al.*, 1985, cited in Hakim, 1987)

- The trade union mark-up on earnings (Chowdhury and Nickell, 1985, cited in Hakim, 1987)
- The causes of marital breakdown (Ross and Sawhill, 1975, cited in Hakim, 1987)

A prospective longitudinal study design examines the prevalence of an outcome in the future; for example, to determine the association between adverse psychosocial characteristics at work and the risk of coronary heart disease among males and females (Kumar, 2005). In that case, participants are asked to give information about themselves and their circumstances on several different occasions. A prospective longitudinal study explores change in the future, and it can study either the same population or different samples at various intervals (Bowling, 2014). In other words, a prospective longitudinal study investigates a sample or group and follows it up, with repeated data collections, over a long period of time (Hakim, 1987).

Another type of longitudinal study is the retrospective study design, which investigates what happened in the past with data available from that period or based on the recollection of that situation by study participants, for example, to examine the risk of cardiovascular events experienced by patients with end-stage renal disease undergoing haemodialysis (Stefánsson *et al.*, 2014). However, information on attitudes, values and motivations can only be collected regarding the present, and retrospective information on the reasons behind earlier events (even if collected) are considered to be ambivalent, given the distortions that colour explanations recalled after the event. Explanations given after the event might be distorted by a concern to maintain or restore "face", post hoc rationalisation, or seeking to establish consistency between the past and the present, or between the present and the future (Semin and Manstead, 1983, cited in Hakim, 1987). Retrospective studies are considered to be quasi-longitudinal studies, which usually take a nationally representative sample that is interviewed once only, collecting information retrospectively on education, work, health and family histories in a shortened form (e.g. some surveys ask respondents to provide information from memory on their family situation during childhood and their parent's education, employment and attitudes as a short cut to an inter-generational study). The advantages of using a retrospective study design relate to both cost, since it is cheaper than a prospective study, and duration, as it is considered to be quicker than a prospective study, especially in cases where in-depth information on personal life histories is required (Hakim, 1987).

In addition, one may use a retrospective-prospective study design, which focuses on the past while studying the phenomenon into the future. More specifically, a part of the data is collected retrospectively, by examining past events from existing records before the intervention, and a follow-up is conducted to ascertain the impact of the intervention (Kumar, 2005). Whether retrospective or prospective, different types of longitudinal study can be combined. For example, a study can be prospective, longitudinal and cohort in the sense that it can collect data in the future over a large period of time and focus on subjects born in a specific year or within a specific period of time.

Bowling (2014) stresses the importance of carefully selecting the variables, the groups to be studied and the rationale behind the study periods. The variables should be clearly defined at the beginning, while researchers should have clear research questions and hypotheses in place before collecting data. Such organisation ensures study rigor and better management of the data during the coding and analysis of the results. The groups should be clearly defined so that there is no variability during data collection. If different groups are studied during the various time intervals, the reliability of the results will be jeopardised. A researcher who chooses to study a phenomenon longitudinally should address two important aspects relating to time: first, the rationale for the number of times to measure or study the phenomenon and second, the period between measurements (Bowling, 2014). Such justification would enhance the rigor of a longitudinal study.

As far as qualitative longitudinal data is concerned, this varies among disciplines and depends on research questions. Longitudinal qualitative studies focus on temporality, processes and social change, and often have an implicit theory of social change informing the analyses. The tools most commonly used include repeat interviews or a combination of ethnographic work and interviewing (O'Riely, 2012). Returning to the individuals or field site after a period of time or over several occasions enhances the understanding of life development and social change (Morawska, 2011). Ethnographers return to the field and their (changing) communities over time (ethnographic returning).

Longitudinal qualitative studies are widely used in different disciplines such as sociology, anthropology, psychology, criminology and so forth (Alasuutari *et al.*, 2008). An ethnographer participates, overtly or covertly, in people's daily lives for an extended period of time, watching what happens, listening to what is said, asking questions and collecting any other relevant data (Hammersley and Atkinson, 1995: 1–10, cited in Punch, 2005: 150).

Particular methods used in qualitative longitudinal research are

- Semi-structured or in-depth interviews: interviews that do not impose any a priori categorisation, which might limit the field of inquiry, although a series of questions are predetermined but open-ended with no fixed range of responses (Given, 2008; Punch, 2005).
- Biographical interviews: biography as a research method involves data gathering about a specific individual (living or deceased) and the interpretation of those data in order to create a representation or portrayal of particular aspects of the subject's life and times (Given, 2008).
- Case studies: research strategies that focus on the in-depth, holistic and in-context study of one or more cases, usually using multiple sources of data (Punch, 2005).
- Diaries: diary writing is used for obtaining personal structured responses and recording the routine of everyday processes. Furthermore, a large number of qualitative studies use diary analysis to observe or improve people's practices by tracking their patterns and cycles. Diaries can be in the form of checklists

that can facilitate health professionals in diagnosing patients' symptoms, medication management and so on. Analysis of diaries can be performed using thematic analysis if the researchers have included open-ended questions in diaries or through mixed-method analysis (Given, 2008). A variety of instruments can also be used (visual, play and drawing methods, e.g. pictures, artwork, video, etc.) (Alasuutari *et al.* 2008; Punch, 2005).

Discuss

- How can longitudinal data be analysed effectively?
- Which ways might be helpful in John's case?

Analysis of quantitative and qualitative longitudinal data

Regarding quantitative data analysis, event history modelling is used for determining the relative importance of a number of independent variables or "covariates" for predicting the outcome of a dependent variable. In event history modelling, the dependent variable is not a measurement of an individual attribute but is derived from the occurrence or non-occurrence of an event, which is temporally marked (Alasuutari *et al.*, 2008). One type of event history modelling is Cox regression (Cox, 1972, cited in Alasuutari *et al.*, 2008), which is a method for modelling time-to-event data and allows the inclusion of predictor variables (covariates). Nevertheless, it has some disadvantages: it is relatively inflexible in terms of modelling duration dependence, and it is difficult to incorporate time-varying covariates, so a discrete-time approach is recommended; this imposes a specific format of the data, and a separate unit of analysis is created for each discrete time interval, where each record is equivalent to a person/month or person/year.

The discrete-time approach provides the researcher with the opportunity to include explanatory variables that vary over time, since each year, or month, that an individual is at risk is treated as a separate observation; it also offers the chance to include more than one measure of duration. Another type of analysis of quantitative longitudinal data is repeated measures analysis, which is more often used in psychology to examine which factors may promote change or stability for individuals or what type of effect a particular life event may have on individual functioning. For instance, in the case of cardiovascular research, repeated measurements are used to test the effects of treatments or disease state on the time course of the response (Alasuutari *et al.*, 2008).

Researchers should be very careful when analysing longitudinal data. This is because the change may have been the result of age itself rather than the measured variables. Additionally, the results might be influenced by forces encompassed in the experiences of the cohort, such as an economic crisis, war, political situations and so forth. Another factor to consider is the "response shift", which refers to how participants may change their understanding of a category or variable under study (i.e. health status, eating habits, etc.). Furthermore, the analysis of data should not be confined to the means at the intervals but should pay more attention to the change within the group, in the sense that the researcher should make sure that it is the same people who are answering the questions. If, for example, some people have stopped smoking while others have started, the end means will show no change in behaviour when there is an actual change within the group. As change is complicated to measure and report, the baseline is to measure the change for each participant and then measure the overall change for the sample (Bowling, 2014).

As far as analysis of qualitative longitudinal data is concerned, it is theoretically driven and characterised by a focus on meaning (Alasuutari *et al.*, 2008). A qualitative longitudinal analysis should be vivid and rigorously correct according to time, process and change. Analysis must be conducted throughout time as well as in an integrative manner. In addition, it should be analytic, in the sense that it should include description, analysis and interpretation. It should chronologically record and describe the different kinds of change that occur, to whom they occur, in what and at what time and context they occur, as well as explain the nature and meaning of those changes, or develop a theory with transferability of the study findings to other contexts (Saldana, 2003, cited in Alasuutari, 2008). Furthermore, the analysis must proceed in two directions – horizontally (across themes) and vertically (over time), or between themes and interviews within a single case to trace the development of a theme over time (Thompson and Holland, 2003, cited in Alasuutari, 2008).

John is interested in collecting and analysing quantitative data. To address his research question and test his hypotheses, John is planning to do a prospective longitudinal cohort study. He wants to study men, aged between 45 and 54 years, in two different geographical areas, over a period of 10 years. It is a cohort study because John will focus on a specific age range. The reason is because heart disease in the age cohort 55–64 is more prevalent among men and because the highest incidences in men before the older ages appear in this cohort (Bhatnagar *et al.*, 2014). Therefore, studying people aged 45 to 54 over a 10-year period would provide John with important data to understand the underlying social factors. John is doing a prospective study because he will be examining an outcome (i.e. heart disease) in the future. John will first identify his population, which is all men aged 45 to 54 years from the local registries. According to the size of his population, John will calculate the statistical power of his sample in order to make sure that he will have statistically significant results. Based on this exercise, John decides to randomly select 1000 men within this age range and follow up with them over a period of 10 years. Once they are identified, John will exclude those participants who have a known heart condition, such as angina, heart attack or any diagnosed heart disease. Therefore, John aims to study healthy men who are at risk due to their age and will consider the impact of various social factors by comparing two different geographical areas.

John is planning to study these two cohorts once a year by asking them to fill in the same validated and standardised questionnaires. John is using such questionnaires to help him test his hypotheses and answer his initial research question. To address the question about the prevalence of heart disease in these two cohorts, John will use a questionnaire to record any diagnosed heart conditions over the years. The heart conditions to be recorded are angina, heart attack and diagnosed heart disease. To test his hypotheses, John will use questionnaires that will collect information in relation to alcohol use, eating habits, socioeconomic class (occupation), and knowledge of the health conditions and their causes. To deal with the challenge of measuring change, John is planning to collaborate with an experienced statistician or epidemiologist. John is excited to have finalised his research question, hypotheses and design, but he is concerned about the possible overwhelming process and duration. He also considers any other potential disadvantages of his longitudinal study.

Discuss

- What are the advantages and disadvantages of longitudinal studies?
- What challenges might John face?
- How can he deal with such challenges?

Advantages and disadvantages of using a longitudinal research design

The dominant characteristic of longitudinal research design is that it allows the researcher to study change in a chronic condition over time by obtaining continuous measures, as they tend to be more accurate. Therefore, especially in chronic diseases such as cardiovascular conditions, it gives the researcher the opportunity to detect the risk factors associated with the onset of the disease. After all, the main advantage of longitudinal research design is that it not only detects risk factors but can also use these screening factors as tests. In particular, longitudinal studies that focus on clinical populations can enhance the collection of thorough information on the population under study. In addition, a longitudinal research design can be used when the researcher wishes to study the mechanisms that are related to disease progression, which might be different from factors that predict disease onset (Guralnik and Kritchevsky, 2010). Further, longitudinal research design can record individual differences in order to return to the specific sample and investigate it further after a period of time, simultaneously exploring why those differences occurred (Kumar, 2005).

On the other hand, there are a few disadvantages accompanying this kind of design. Longitudinal study designs are considered to be uneconomical and time consuming, and they require the effort and involvement of many researchers (Robinson *et al.*, 2008). Of great importance is failure to properly design the study by paying attention to the specific causal issues to be addressed and the anticipation of difficulties that might be encountered, and, thus, most longitudinal studies tend to be exploratory or pilot studies (Hakim, 1987). Clearly, the issue of conditioning effect is one of the most important limitations in longitudinal research, in the sense that the same participants participate in the study, which means that they are aware of the procedure, and this could lead to answering without even thinking or even to participants losing interest in the study (Kumar, 2005).

Also of great importance is the problem of attrition. Since participants might choose to withdraw from the study for whatever reason (refusal, cannot be contacted), this would reduce the strength, representativeness and effectiveness of the results due to the increased possibility of missing data (Alasuutari *et al.*, 2008; Hakim, 1987). Sample attrition due to deaths, imprisonment and hospitalisation can be treated as substantive events, and researchers are strongly encouraged to collect this kind of information. Sample attrition could be anticipated through developing research weights or models; bringing new members on board; oversampling specific groups either through the use of tokens; giving participants the opportunity to choose the way that they would like to be interviewed; collecting the addresses of their significant others rather than the address of the participants themselves in order to trace them; or regular follow-up of the personal details of the participants and, especially, their home address (Olsen, 2005, cited in Alasuutari *et al.*, 2008).

There is also the possibility that the questions addressed at the beginning of the study may be overtaken by events or may be discussed by other studies, previously completed, that focus on the same issue (Hakim, 1987). Another issue raised is the problem of causality, since observational longitudinal studies can give evidence for, but not clearly state, the causes for the phenomenon under study (Guralnik and Kritchevsky, 2010). However, a longitudinal study design can help the researcher understand the possible causal relationships between variables, since it takes omitted variables into account through the development of models that can take into consideration the complexities of the social world as well as the influences on an individual's behaviour (Alasuutari *et al.*, 2008).

Importantly, other threats to validity in longitudinal research designs are instrumentation and regression to the mean. Instrumentation refers to the instrument used, which could be different each time for different ages, or could be the same and the interpretations could differ, or could limit the generalisability of the results. Another issue is that researchers or research assistants could moderate their attitude to the research across time, and this could affect the whole research procedure. Also, variables could change over time, as well as the theoretical framework on which the whole study is based, and researchers need to reconsider them over time (Robinson *et al.*, 2008).

Regarding regression to the mean, this statistical phenomenon seems to appear when repeated measures occur, as well as when error variance decreases over time, as reliability increases and researchers must examine variance over time (Buss, 1979, cited in Robinson *et al.*, 2008). One way to anticipate this problem is to draw independent samples at each time of testing (Kosloski, 1986, cited in Robinson *et al.*, 2008). A major ethical consideration that arises from longitudinal research is the distortion of life experience when repeated interventions are implemented. In addition, confidentiality is of major concern, since the collection of in-depth information in a continuous form would be more likely to lead to the disclosure of participants' identity (Alasuutari *et al.* 2008).

Weighing the above-mentioned advantages and disadvantages, John is more confident that a longitudinal study design can help him to understand the course of heart conditions in two different geographical areas and to understand the relevant influential social factors. His major concern is the required resources and time for the successful completion of such an endeavour. To deal with this challenge, John is applying to local authorities, universities and funding agencies in order to secure funding for his research. His main goal is to have enough financial resources to employ research assistants for the data collection and its subsequent analysis.

Conclusion

Overall, longitudinal studies should be designed in relation to large-scale studies (Campbell, 1988, cited in Robinson *et al.*, 2008). Furthermore, it is suggested that they should be planned in relation to the available funding and researchers should be able to collect additional data on participants as well as provide extensive training to the staff who will collect the data. "Blind testing" could also be introduced in longitudinal surveys in order to build rapport with participants and reduce bias. Additionally, regarding the staff turnover that might occur due to the length of time that the study takes, this could be anticipated by publishing findings, even if this requires publishing preliminary data that might impact subsequent behaviours (van der Kamp and Bijleved, 1998, cited in Robinson *et al.*, 2008).

References

Alasuutari P, Bickman L and Brannen J (2008) *The SAGE Handbook of Social Research Methods*. London: SAGE.

Albus, C (2010) Psychological and social factors in coronary heart disease. *Annals of Medicine* 42: 487–494.

Bhatnagar P, Wickramasinghe K, Williams J, Rayner M and Townsend N (2015) The epidemiology of cardiovascular disease in the UK 2014. *Heart* 101:1182–1189.

Bowling A (2014) *Research Methods in Health: Investigating Health and Health Services* (4th ed.). London: McGraw-Hill.

Bryman A and Teevan, JJ (2005) *Social Research Methods*. New York: Oxford University Press.

Given LM (2008) *The Sage Encyclopedia of Qualitative Research Methods*. London: SAGE.

Guralnik JM and Kritchevsky SB (2010) Translating research to promote health aging: The complementary role of longitudinal studies and clinical trials. *Journal of the American Geriatric Society* 2: 337–342.

Hakim C (1987) *Research Design. Strategies and Choices in the Design of Social Research*. London: Routledge.

Kreatsoulas C and Anand SS (2010) The impact of social determinants on cardiovascular disease. *Canadian Journal of Cardiology* 26: 8C–13C.

Kumar R (2005) *Research Methodology: A Step-by-Step Guide for Beginners*. London: SAGE.

Morawska E (2011) Studying international migration in the long (er) and short (er) durée: Contesting some and reconciling other disagreements between the structuration and morphogenetic approaches. International Migration Institute Working Papers Series, No. 44, Oxford.

O'Reilly K (2012) Ethnographic returning, qualitative longitudinal research and the reflexive analysis of social practice. *The Sociological Review* 60(3): 518–536.

Perk J, De Backer G, Gohlke H, Graham I, Reiner Z and Verschuren WM (2012) European guidelines on cardiovascular disease prevention in clinical practice: The fifth joint task force of the European society of cardiology and other societies on cardiovascular disease prevention in clinical practice (constituted by representatives of nine societies and by invited experts). *International Journal of Behavioural Medicine* 19(4): 403–488.

Powell-Wiley TM, Cooper-McCann R, Ayers C, Berrigan D, Lian M and McClurkin M (2015). Change in Neighborhood Socioeconomic Status and Weight Gain Dallas Heart Study. *American Journal of Preventive Medicine* 49(1): 72–79.

Punch KF (2005) *Introduction to Social Research: Quantitative and Qualitative Approaches*. London: SAGE.

Robinson K, Schmidt T, Teti DM (2008) Issues in the Use of the Longitudinal and Cross-Sectional Designs. Handbook of Research Methods in Developmental Science. Oxford, UK: Blackwell Publishing.

Schnohr P, Marott JL, Kristensen TS, Gyntelberg F, Grønbæk M and Lange P (2015) Ranking of psychosocial and traditional risk factors by importance for coronary heart disease: The Copenhagen City Heart Study. *European Heart Journal* 36(22): 1385–1393.

Stefánsson BV, Brunelli SM, Cabrera C, Rosenbaum D, Anum E and Ramakrishnan K (2014) Intradialytic hypotension and risk of cardiovascular disease. *Clinical Journal of the American Society of Nephrology* 9(12): 2124–2132.

World Health Organization (2015). Cardiovascular Diseases (CVDs), Fact sheet No. 317. Available online at: www.who.int/mediacentre/factsheets/fs317/en/. Accessed 12 December 2015.

7 Using the Internet

HIV/AIDS

Abstract

Dr Frank Stevenson, a researcher, is interested in studying people who live with HIV/AIDS in London. While there are quite a few quantitative and qualitative studies on patients with HIV/AIDS, Dr Stevenson wants to focus on married men and explore the changes in their lives and any incidents of stigmatisation they might have experienced. Interestingly, though he finds potential participants, he finds that it is difficult to persuade them to participate. Patients are afraid of public exposure even though Dr Stevenson assures them of confidentiality.

This chapter presents the experiences of people with HIV/AIDS as they have been documented by various research studies and presents the Internet as a tool for conducting research from a distance and keeping the participants' personal information confidential.

Learning objectives:

- Describe the experiences of people living with HIV/AIDS through the literature review.
- Describe the procedure of conducting research using the Internet.
- Outline the advantages and disadvantages of using the Internet to conduct research on public health issues.

Scenario

Dr Frank Stevenson, a researcher, is interested in studying people who live with HIV/AIDS in London. While there are quite a few quantitative and qualitative studies on patients with HIV/AIDS, Frank wants to focus on married men and explore the changes in their lives after the diagnosis and any incidents of stigmatisation they might have experienced. This decision is also driven by convenience, as he does not expect to find many potential participants to take part in a quantitative study. However, the potential participants he finds are reluctant to participate in his study out of fear of public exposure even though Frank assures them of complete anonymity and confidentiality. It seems that the fear of stigmatisation is more powerful than confidentiality itself. Frank is disappointed, but he does not want to give up his idea, as he would like to understand more about his potential participants' way of thinking. He delves into the relevant literature to learn more about how people with HIV/AIDS experience their condition, and this enables him to refine his research question and come up with ideas regarding ways in which to persuade prospective research participants to take part in the study.

Discuss

- How could the literature help Frank?
- What could the literature show Frank about people living with HIV/AIDS?
- Could information about people living with HIV/AIDS help Frank with his research question and research methodology? In which ways?

The lived experience of people living with HIV/AIDS

Numerous research papers, using different methodologies, have been used in order to explore the lived experience of people living with HIV/AIDS (Côté *et al.*, 2015; Highton and Finn, 2015; Kako *et al.*, 2013; Malave *et al.*, 2014). More specifically, a survey conducted by Malave *et al.* (2014) in India aimed to describe gender differences to the experience of living with HIV, with 159 men and 154 women recruited from non-governmental organisations in India. The study found that the lived experience varies between genders. For instance, men reported significantly higher mean levels of internalised stigma. In addition, various life transitions due to the HIV diagnosis were also described in a different form by women and men. More women reported moving out of their homes, whereas more men (89 per cent) than women (66 per cent) reported an alteration to their sexual behaviour after the HIV diagnosis.

Furthermore, a longitudinal qualitative study informed by post-colonial feminism was conducted in the USA with a sample of 54 women (Kako *et al.*, 2013), aiming to explore the lived experience of living with HIV and stigma. This revealed that the stigma of HIV had made others treat people with HIV as outsiders and that they had been labelled as possessing deviant behaviour. The experience of diagnosis seemed to be a devastating event that produced feelings of despair and depression among individuals. The second theme related to the various methods used by women to resist socially constructed stigma mainly by keeping their HIV status a secret.

In a mixed method study in Canada (Côté *et al.*, 2015), with 24 subjects (81 per cent being male), aiming to describe the psychosocial profile and lived experience of HIV-infected long-term non-progressors, results showed a modest mean score for social support. The qualitative part of the study revealed a variety of changes that people with HIV had to make in relation to their illness: specifically, modification of their lifestyle (smoking, alcohol, healthy diet, exercise, etc.) and changing their sexual behaviour (engaging in safe sex).

A qualitative research study in the UK (Highton and Finn, 2015), which used Foucauldian-informed discourse analysis in order to explore the lived experience of HIV positive, heterosexual fathers living in London through semi-structured face-to-face interviews, revealed several changes in those men's lives after the diagnosis. These included major adjustments towards their expectations and ambitions, work losses and a change related to their sense of self. Further, participants described that there is a social perception that HIV-positive heterosexual men are the ones to blame for their illness, since they were more likely to be engaged in promiscuous sex (Highton and Finn, 2015).

A 2005 study conducted by the Research Unit in Behavioural and Social Issues (RUBSI) in Cyprus aimed to describe the social and psychological needs of people living with HIV in Cyprus. Fifty people filled in a self-completed questionnaire in relation to their experience of living with HIV as well as their needs and how they addressed those needs. Furthermore, five semi-structured interviews were carried out with key persons involved with HIV/AIDS in Cyprus, and two seminars/workshops were conducted. The study revealed that 40 per cent of the participants were refused employment because they were HIV positive, while 30 per cent faced social discrimination and 30 per cent had experienced problems with their families because of their HIV status. Overall, 75 per cent of respondents declared that they had faced discrimination on account of ignorance/lack of information regarding issues of transmission; the media; medical personnel and homophobia.

Moreover, a study conducted in the USA (Baumgartner, 2004), aiming to investigate the experiences of 12 African American men living with HIV/AIDS through semi-structured interviews, revealed that stigma inhibited support, education and treatment, and led to the experience of double stigmatisation (due to being Black and HIV positive). Another issue that was found to be related to stigma was race in relation to treatment. Moreover, heterosexual men experienced the diagnosis as a death sentence.

Discuss

- How can this information be helpful to Frank?
- Could Frank still try to use qualitative interviews to collect data? If not, what other ways could he consider?

Frank recognises that HIV/AIDS is not a mere medical condition, which can be managed by medication. It reaches out to encompass the individual as a social being, as well as the family and the whole community. It is a condition that carries symbolic connotations that can change a patient's way of thinking as well as his or her social life. Franks wants to study an even more sensitive aspect. That is, being married might have had a greater impact on a patient's social life because it implies that the patient contracted the condition after having had extra-marital sexual relations. The literature helps Frank to refine his research question to the following: How has the life of married patients with HIV changed and what stigmatisation has the patient experienced since their HIV diagnosis?

Knowing the sensitivity of the issue, Frank is still faced with a practical challenge: how can he find research participants? Since HIV/AIDS is a sensitive and stigmatising condition, potential participants who were married at the time of diagnosis may be even more reluctant to participate in such a study. Frank wonders whether there are other ways to collect data and considers using the Internet as a possible tool. As the Internet is widely used nowadays, potential participants may be more willing to express their experiences without having to meet with any researchers. Frank tries to find out more about the use of the Internet in research studies.

Conducting research using the Internet

The Internet can be a useful tool for conducting research, and there are certain ways to use the Internet for this purpose. More specifically, the Internet can be used as a resource locator, for completing demographic surveys and for empirical investigations (Senior, 1999, cited in Ahern, 2005). The best-known way is the recruitment of participants through the Internet and directing them to an online site where a discussion board or a survey is available. Data are then transmitted to the researcher via e-mail or through data files maintained by the webserver (Eaton *et al*., 2002).

A study was conducted by O'Brien *et al.* (2014) to describe how researchers developed and administered an instrument called the HIV, Health and Rehabilitation Survey. The instrument was developed by the research team and was based on a literature review. Afterwards, it was reviewed, revised and pretested three times by the entire team, which involved all team members independently reviewing the questionnaire for content, clarity and format. Before this, members of the research team living with HIV completed the questionnaire as potential participants, and a meeting followed in order to review the content, format and administration of the survey instrument and to finalise the recruitment process prior to implementation. The survey was administered electronically via five community organisations using a modified Dillman Tailored Design Method, whereby eligible participants were those who had access to the Internet and e-mail. An initial e-mail invitation was first circulated to clients and then a reminder followed. The researchers underlined that

- The software was easy to use
- The questionnaire could be completed at the participants' own time and pace
- The administration of the online survey had given the researchers the opportunity to obtain geographic variation
- Participation in the study was anonymous

On the other hand, the researchers underlined some considerations for future survey implementation, including

- Respondent burden and fatigue
- The potentially sensitive nature of HIV web-based research
- Data management and storage

- The challenge of verifying informed consent
- Varying computer skills among respondents
- The burden of community organisations (O'Brien *et al.*, 2014)

In psychology, three types of methods are used for conducting Internet research: translational methods, phenomenological methods and novel methods. Translational methods refer to using the Internet to conduct more traditional studies, such as surveys, face-to-face interviews and experiments. Phenomenological methods are studies that use the Internet to make sense of users' conscious behaviour. For example, bullying in an online forum could be a topic of phenomenological interest. Novel methods are the new ways psychologists have to study phenomena via the Internet, which have been difficult to study on a large scale, such as the study of secrets or rumours (Gosling and Mason, 2014). Overall, the Internet, as a tool for conducting research, can facilitate the preparation of research studies, the development of research methodologies and the location of resources.

Frank is excited to know that the Internet has been used as a means to conduct qualitative research. He considers constructing a semi-structured questionnaire for interviews and envisions using an online forum/space where he can pose questions to his participants without having to see them. However, he is uncertain about the practicalities of such an endeavour, as well as any ethical issues that might derive from this activity. He examines the existing literature to learn more.

Discuss

- What should Frank pay attention to when examining the literature?
- What method of recruitment might be helpful to adequately address his research question?

Recruitment of participants

According to Gosling and Mason (2014), there are four methods for the online recruitment of research participants: delivery to standard populations, respondent-driven sampling, delivery to target populations, and crowdsourcing (Gosling and Mason, 2014).

Delivery to standard populations

Delivery to standard populations refers to the distribution of questionnaires to participants through the web (Kraut *et al.*, 2004). Researchers often use online panels or groups of people who have volunteered to be contacted for online research, thus allowing the researcher to have a more reliable pool of participants, as well as facilitating the collection of longitudinal data that otherwise might have been expensive or difficult to obtain (Goritz, 2004).

Respondent-driven sampling

Researchers may be assisted by other Internet users to find participants. This is named "respondent-driven sampling" because the recruitment of participants is done through word of mouth, via social media and other information channels (Goritz, 2004). This might be a very useful method because it can emphasise the importance of the study and encourage more people to participate. It resembles a snowball method in conventional recruitment but it can happen at a large scale.

Delivery to targeted populations

Delivery to targeted populations is used when targeting populations that are hard to reach via conventional means. Therefore, it helps to recruit populations via online forums and interest groups, as well as through online advertisements. In addition, researchers can use the Internet to target participants (e.g. bloggers, tweeters), even if they have not self-selected into specialist groups. Imagine a researcher who wants to contact people who are interested in a topic or, from a specific location, could search for users posting on that topic in that location using tags (e.g. Instagram) or other search engines. Alternatively, researchers could advertise their studies via Facebook, where participants can be targeted using certain features (e.g. demographics, geographic location and preferences via likes). Moreover, targeting strategies can also be useful for identifying relevant existing data, to examine patterns of behaviour, feelings, thoughts and social connections expressed by people who belong to a specific group. For example, a study conducted by Wolf *et al.* (2013) compared the content of pro-eating disorder blogs, recovery blogs and control blogs. In addition, Ritter *et al.* (2014) explored the role of thinking styles and social connections as meanings behind the tendency for Christians to be happier than atheists. This was done through two million tweets from over 16,000 Twitter users who followed either Christian or atheist leaders. The researchers showed that intuitive (versus analytic) thinking style and frequency of words related to social relationships partially mediated the higher levels of happiness of Christians relative to atheists.

In the case of participants who are HIV positive, who often participate in risk-taking behaviours that are stigmatized or illegal, this may lead to the formation of "hidden subpopulations" that are crucial to preventing the spread of HIV (Magnani *et al.*, 2005). Therefore, social networks on the Internet enable the recruitment of these "hidden subpopulations" through a snowball sampling strategy and by advertising on targeted interest (e.g. MSM) blogs and message boards, as well as drug use, dating and social networking sites, such as Grindr, Facebook, Adam4Adam, Bluelight and DrugsForum.com (Bowen *et al.*, 2004).

Thus, the increased reach and coverage have given HIV researchers access to hard-to-reach subgroups of people. However, ethical issues are raised in relation to sample recruitment via the Internet that relate to privacy, confidentiality and informed consent. When it comes to privacy and confidentiality, using social networking sites for recruiting subjects into HIV studies raises issues related to lack of confidentiality when evaluation data are collected online, poor user privacy and confidentiality protections of social networking sites, and threats related to the collection of protected health information. To anticipate the ethical issues raised, especially in the case of HIV participants, it is recommended that identifiable data should only be accessible to the research team, ID numbers could be assigned to participants offline, and all online information about participants could be accessed via this number. Also, the research team should avoid inviting participants to be their online "friends" or to "like" them. In this way, they will not have access to personal information on profile pages and can only access information that participants make publicly available. In addition, the "contact us" and/or "sign up" request should not be located on social networking sites, and in the case that researchers would like participants to sign up or to invite their friends to participate, the research team should direct potential participants to a site landing page that is secure and not connected to the social networking site.

In cases when participants are not allowed to post information to the study's social networking site, postings must be monitored multiple times each day and all identifiable or inappropriate information should be removed. Furthermore, regular reviews of the site's privacy, confidentiality policies, and advertiser, business and third party features should be performed. Apart from this, in the case of collecting health information (Health Insurance Portability and Accountability Act [HIPAA]), all assessments should be collected through secured Internet sites that are not housed by social networking sites, while the storage and transfer of electronic data must use current standards of encryption and password protection and should be stored behind a secure firewall.

In general, in relation to informed consent, it is easier when using the Internet for participants to declare a false age. When it comes to voluntary participation, the researcher must ensure that participants can withdraw from the study at any time they wish; this could be facilitated by creating a withdraw button (Hewson, 2003). Confidentiality is also threatened when using the Internet; for example, when trying to send an email response, if by mistake the email is sent to another recipient other than the one it was intended for, then the data submitted will be viewed by a third party. There is also the possibility of hacking (Hewson, 2003).

Lastly, the issue of debriefing might be difficult to implement when using the Internet. Several methods are used to implement debriefing. This could be done via a debriefing text that includes the explanation of the study aims and objectives as well as contact details for further information about the procedure and the study in general, even though this should not necessary lead to the conclusion that the participant has actually read the debriefing note (Hewson, 2003).

Some recommendations were made in order to anticipate all the ethical issues raised when using the Internet to conduct research (Szabo and Frenkl, 1996, cited in Hewson, 2003). These include minimising the demographic information requested and avoiding selection of the participants based on ethnicity, religion, income, occupation or sexual preferences. In general, it was declared that studies that address those issues should not be conducted via the internet. Nevertheless, as already mentioned, it is necessary to gather demographic information from participants to avoid sampling biases, evaluate different sampling procedures and address issues of data validity (Hewson, 2003). As has been stated, the most important advantage of Internet research is that it provides access to special interest populations and minority groups.

Crowdsourcing

Crowdsourcing websites are online marketplaces that help to create tasks in line with the requesters, compensating the workers and rating the quality of the requests and worker performance. Requesters can create and virtually post any task that can be done at a computer (i.e. surveys, experiments, writing, etc.) through simple templates or technical scripts or linking workers to external online survey tools (e.g. Survey Monkey). Then, workers can browse available tasks and are paid upon the successful completion of each task. As far as the analysis is concerned, there are also different methods reported. That is, the analysis could be passive, such that the information patterns on websites or interactions on discussion groups take place without the researcher's involvement. Alternatively, the analysis could be active in the sense that the researcher participates in the communication. Moreover, researchers could be involved in data collection (Eysenbach *et al.*, 2001).

Discuss

- Which recruitment method might be more suitable in Frank's case?
- Could Frank use multiple methods to recruit his participants?

Frank has a sensitive research question to address and a difficult group of participants to recruit. He is planning to use one method as the backbone for identifying participants. His main method will be "delivery to targeted populations" to advertise his research and an invitation to participate through online communities of people with HIV/AIDS. Within these communities, Frank hopes to find patients who were married at the time of diagnosis. To recruit his participants, Frank has a specific step-by-step plan based on the relevant literature. First, Frank must be honest with his potential participants and inform them that he is a social researcher who wants to explore the experiences of married patients with HIV/AIDS. Frank will not pretend that he is a patient himself. Second, he will have a short and clear online description of his research topic and aims. In the description of the study, Frank will have a paragraph about the potential benefit for this group of participants. That is, the study may show the need for the more systematic education of society regarding HIV/AIDS and more support for patients so as to be able to manage their condition and cope with the stigma they may be facing. Third, he will invite his participants to follow a link to enter a specially arranged online room, which only he and his participants can access. Fourth, upon joining the online room and before starting the interviews, his participants will have the opportunity to read a short and clear informed consent form and press an "I accept" button. In the informed consent form, Frank will have a clear sentence about the participants' right not to answer any of the questions and to withdraw at any time they wish or to withdraw any of their answers. By doing so, Frank ensures confidentiality and deals with ethical issues that may derive from such an online study. Fifth, the interview will take place on paper, in the sense that Frank will not see or hear his participants but rather, will ask questions and receive the answers in writing. Though this will take a lot of time, participants will have the opportunity to read their replies before sending them to Frank. Also, Frank will save a lot of time by not having to transcribe the interviews.

For the time being, Frank does not want to use other methods to recruit participants, such as advertising to social media or respondent-driven methods, because he does not want to make his research too public and eventually scare off potential participants. He may reconsider using these methods in the event that he does not find enough participants for his study. Even though publicising his topic may deter potential participants from participating, it might work the other way around, making the topic seem more important and timely and, thus, encouraging more people to participate.

Discuss

- What are the advantages and disadvantages of using online interviews?
- What other methods of collecting data might be appropriate in Frank's case?

Methods for collecting data through the Internet

There are a few methods for collecting data through the Internet. These include Internet-based surveys, questionnaires, interviews, virtual focus groups, observation, experiments, reviewing materials posted on the Internet and Intervention Studies. Let us consider these methods one by one to consider what is best for Frank's study.

Internet-based surveys

Internet-based surveys are the most common methodology used in Internet research. They can be conducted online through interactive surveys and can be completed and submitted directly to the researcher or with survey forms that are downloaded and then e-mailed or faxed to the researcher. In addition, within chat rooms or via e-mail, one-to-one interviews between the researcher and the participant may also take place. Surveys that are mailed back to the researcher have the advantage that they can be anonymous with only some demographics written on the envelope (e.g. city). However, surveys sent by fax can be traced to the phone line from which they originated, since fax numbers appear on the received fax. E-mail responses can also threaten to uncover the participant's identity (Fitzpatrick and Montgomery, 2004).

Another danger associated with Internet-based surveys is the scientific status of the researcher conducting the survey; for example, if the person is a student he or she may not be viewed seriously and the participant may choose not to participate. Also, reliability and validity issues arise, and the literature proposes the use of a paper-version questionnaire as a follow-up. To confront any problems or misinterpretations that might have occurred among subjects who completed the online survey, researchers need to provide a feedback mechanism via e-mail or other means or via the use of time stamps from the participants when they complete the surveys (Fitzpatrick and Montgomery, 2004).

Questionnaires

Questionnaires are the most versatile and broadly used tools in Internet research and they do not require a great deal of technical knowhow in order to be used. Questionnaires can be uploaded onto an already existing website and, of course, can include numerous questions (Hewson, 2003).

Interviews

Internet interviews can provide anonymity; however, the ability to observe verbal and non-verbal communication cues is diminished. An Internet-based interview can be conducted via e-mail, whereby the researcher sends a set of questions to the interviewee, who then replies via e-mail. The whole procedure facilitates follow-up questions or clarifications on the answers already given and gives the interviewee the opportunity to answer at a time that is convenient to them, as well as giving them the opportunity to answer questions thoroughly, thus increasing the validity of answers given. Overall, it provides the opportunity for interaction between the interviewer and interviewee in an online chat room (Hewson, 2003).

However, there are some limitations identified in the literature concerning this type of online data collection method, which mainly concern the role of the interviewer/researcher in qualitative research and the mutual interaction between the participant and the researcher (Fitzpatrick and Montgomery, 2004).

Virtual focus groups

Virtual focus groups can be conducted in an extended period of time compared with traditional focus groups that are usually covered in one or two sessions (depending on the number of participants), while participants may not interact with each other or the researcher directly (Fitzpatrick and Montgomery,2004).

Observation studies

A type of observation called *indirect observation* can be used online. This relates mainly to the observation of archived postings to newsgroups. In addition, the Internet provides the opportunity to examine non-linguistic aspects of behaviour through the presentation of problem-solving or decision-making tasks, simulation in observing behaviour, constructing games or role playing through an online interaction with a computer programme (Hewson, 2003).

Experiments

Several types of experiments can be conducted via the Internet, including experiments that include printed text or graphics, experiments that include video or sound, reaction-time experiments, and experiments involving interpersonal interaction. Despite the various advantages that this type of research has, there is also a need to have a homogeneous presentation of the format of materials for all participants. Nevertheless, there are some problems involved with the creation of HTML files when using different browsers, such as Netscape Navigator or Internet Explorer, which could threaten data validity. This could be addressed through prior testing of the experimental materials before making them available online. Additionally, the file size can make participants discontinue the experiment before completing it. This could also be minimised by pretesting in order to control the time required for files to be downloaded. Moreover, using extended video files can be time consuming, so it is essential to keep files to a manageable size, although this could affect the presentation of the materials (Hewson, 2003).

Another issue that researchers should take into account is the use of different devices and, consequently, the different way that material may appear to the participants, therefore affecting its quality. This could be managed by trying to run the material at an optimum level on the slowest device to identify the minimum hardware requirements needed to run the experiment adequately. As far as reaction time experiments – those that require exact measurements – are concerned, certain problems can arise, especially when using the Internet to implement them, since participants would use several platforms and Internet connection speeds, which could lead to inaccuracies in measurement. This could be avoided by downloading the program to the participant's computer (Hewson, 2003).

Lastly, another type of experiment, which is based on interactions between participants through interactive chat, does not consider non-verbal communication when conducted online. However, Internet users have developed a system of symbolic representations, such as facial expressions, that can help in overcoming this limitation (Hewson, 2003).

Reviewing materials posted on a webpage

This method of data collection is considered to be essential to understanding people and the social and cultural contexts in which they live and allows the investigation of participants beyond the experimental settings. Furthermore, it helps researchers gain a bigger picture about health beliefs, common topics of discussion, as well as motivational and emotional needs. However, some ethical issues might arise, since "participants" are not aware that they are participating in a research study (Fitzpatrick and Montgomery, 2004).

Intervention studies

Internet-based intervention methods include interventions that are provided online and studies in which participants are randomised to the intervention group, which includes an Internet component (Fitzpatrick and Montgomery, 2004).

In conclusion, Frank is even more confident now that using online interviews is the best way for collecting rich data for the in-depth understanding of his participants' experiences. Though Frank will lose valuable information from verbal and non-verbal communication, as the information exchange will solely be in writing, it seems that it is a good way to answer his sensitive research question.

Discuss

- How could Frank analyse his data?
- Is the analysis of online interviews different from the analysis of conventional interviews? How so?

Analysis of online data

The analysis of online data is similar to the analysis of conventional data. Quantitative data can be inserted into Excel for the simplest questionnaires, while the results from more complicated online questionnaires can be entered into statistical software to check for correlations and statistical significance. Another analysis technique is data mining, which extracts knowledge from data based on artificial intelligence and statistical techniques using computers. With researcher guidance, the computer program builds models to assist in explaining complex relationships. In the case of healthcare, data mining is being used to predict clinical outcomes, such as disease survival rates and health outcomes (Fitzpatrick and Montgomery, 2004). Additionally, secondary data analysis can be performed through the use of existing Internet databases, which reduces the cost and time of collecting primary data (secondary data analysis is further discussed in Chapter 8).

The same applies to qualitative data, which is what Frank will be analysing. Frank will not have to transcribe the interviews because he will have the answers in writing; however, he will have to code and categorise the data. It would be easier for Frank if he organised his questions in accordance with his research question to ensure a good interview structure and to facilitate categorisation. Though Frank will have the chance to pose additional questions, which may derive from the interview, a structured interview can work as a pre-coding/categorisation of data framework. Frank will also need to consider saturation of data to make sure that he has enough information to adequately address his research question (Guest *et al.*, 2006). If he does not achieve saturation, he will need to continue recruiting participants (saturation of data in interviews and how to achieve this is covered more thoroughly in Chapter 3).

> **Discuss**
>
> - What should Frank consider now before deciding to use the Internet?
> - Could the use of the Internet have serious drawbacks, which could potentially deter researchers from proceeding?

Advantages and disadvantages of using the Internet to conduct research

There are many advantages when using the Internet to conduct research. First, the associated cost is lower than that of surveys that are completed using paper and pencil (Rhodes *et al.*, 2003; Roos, 2003). Second, Internet sampling has been proven to be time-saving (Fitzpatrick and Montgomery, 2004). Third, Internet research provides the ability to reach an extended number of participants, which improves the external reliability and generalisability of the sample (Meyerson, 2003; Pittenger, 2003; Rhodes *et al.*, 2003). However, one must take into consideration the different linguistic and political orientations that might exist and create different versions of the tool that can be used for different audiences (Fitzpatrick and Montgomery, 2004). Fourth are access issues, since it provides an opportunity for researchers to access sensitive populations and cultural groups as well as hidden populations (Pittenger, 2003; Rhodes *et al.*, 2003; Stickland *et al.*, 2003). Fifth is methodological rigour and control by the researcher (Granello *et al.*, 2003). Sixth is the accuracy and efficiency of data entry and data analysis (Granello *et al.*, 2003; Rhodes *et al.*, 2003; Stewart, 2003; Wilson, 2003). Seventh is the provision of conducting follow-up studies as well as the obtaining of additional response-set information and feedback (Granello *et al.*, 2003; Rhodes *et al.*, 2003).

In addition, there are some advantages reported in relation to the study participants, such as

- The provision of anonymity (Bowker *et al.*, 2004; Gosling *et al.*, 2004) and the advantage of having an interactive communication that can be either synchronous (several people on the Internet at the same time communicating simultaneously) or asynchronous (the researcher posts questions anytime, anywhere and then the participant can answer the questions at another time or place) (Fitzpatrick and Montgomery, 2004).
- The provision of the ability to respond at their own pace when they find it appropriate to do so (Bowker *et al.*, 2004; Rhodes *et al.*, 2003).
- The perception of control (Barry, 2001).
- The perception that it is a more fascinating way of conducting research (Barry, 2001).
- The straightforwardness of use (Rhodes *et al.*, 2003; Roos, 2003).

The international literature also maintains that it could be used as an educational tool for students (Rhodes *et al.*, 2003).

However, there are also some limitations reported that can be considered to be disadvantages to the use of the specific methodology. First, it diminishes internal validity, since there is no control over the test setting (Birnbhaum, 2004; Daley *et al.*, 2003; Eaton *et al.*, 2002; Pittenger, 2003). Taking this into consideration, a pilot study must precede the main study; researchers might ask a listserv group or a chat room to evaluate the pilot survey (Fitzpatrick and Montgomery, 2004). Second, it diminishes external validity because there seems to be bias in relation to recruitment, since this is done through the self-selection of participants from a non-random pool of computer/Internet users. Also, there is the possibility that online participant recruitment may miss lower socioeconomic and otherwise marginalised groups and potentially result in a non-representative sample. To prevent bias, one needs to first screen possible participants and then send the survey to selected participants. Potential participants could be screened based on demographic or other criteria. When participants are pre-screened, the researcher will eventually have more control over who completes the survey. For intervention studies, participants must first be asked whether they have a health/medical condition that is changing and whether they need to see a healthcare provider for treatment (Fitzpatrick and Montgomery, 2004).

Third, there might be problems with the electronic equipment as well as the network (Birnbaum, 2004; Hewson, 2003). In such a case, the survey could be sent multiple times and data could be collected over an extended period of time in order to increase the chances of the survey reaching subjects. Also, in the case that devices and networks are available to family members or co-workers, multiple individuals could complete and submit the survey or access what the original subject answered (Fitzpatrick and Montgomery, 2004). Fourth, the creation and maintenance of a user-friendly website is time consuming (Daley *et al.*, 2003; Stewart, 2003; Wilson, 2003). Fifth, there is doubt about the response rate. Sixth, a survey error might also occur due to complex design. It is suggested that researchers keep the online survey easy to read and easy to load and, at the same time, take into consideration the participants' developmental level and any special needs they may have. Also, larger fonts (14 points and higher) are recommended for use with older individuals, as well as highly contrasting fonts and backgrounds that would make the text easier to read (e.g. black type on white backgrounds); webpage colours should be carefully selected, and so on. Also, surveys could be sent within the body of an e-mail rather than as attachments, thereby making them easier for participants to access (Fitzpatrick and Montgomery, 2004).

Seventh, the authenticity of the participants' data is disputed, since there might be multiple submissions by the same participant (Birnbhaum, 2004; Bowker *et al.*, 2004; Gosling *et al.*, 2004). In that case, the researcher needs to create a unique way of identifying each participant. For example, if the researcher is using a database, such as an organisational list of names and e-mails, a unique member number may be helpful. Additionally, the researcher could have another person filtering responses and checking for multiple submissions and false responses by comparing identical demographic information and answers on surveys using a computer statistical program. Bogus answers include items that do not correspond to the question asked or that contain letters or numbers that do not communicate meaningful information (Fitzpatrick and Montgomery, 2004). Eighth, there is limited international scope (Rhodes *et al.*, 2003) and ninth, there is competition for attention (Rhodes *et al.*, 2003). Tenth, there are barriers in relation to Internet credibility (Duffy, 2000); eleventh, potential data entry errors (Im *et al.*, 2004); and, finally, obscure public and private boundaries on the Internet in relation to privacy and confidentiality issues (Bowker *et al.*, 2004; Im *et al.*, 2004; Pittenger, 2003; Rhodes *et al.*, 2003; Stewart, 2003; Wilson, 2003).

Frank decides that the advantages are more important than the disadvantages when studying such a sensitive topic. Furthermore, Frank considers that most of the important disadvantages can be easily addressed. More specifically, validity can be satisfied though achieving data saturation, while confidentiality can be ensured through the systematic approach presented earlier in this chapter. Frank cannot guarantee that his participants are indeed patients with HIV/AIDS or/and were married at the time of diagnosis. Though this might be a serious drawback, it can easily occur in more conventional qualitative studies. Another limitation is that Frank will miss non-verbal cues. However, despite their importance, they are typically omitted in conventional studies due to the overwhelming amount of data that can derive from qualitative interviews.

Conclusion

HIV/AIDS-related stigma remains a potent stressor for HIV-positive people. This chapter examined the relationships among stigma-related experiences and depression, self-confidence, discrimination and self-esteem among heterosexual married men living with HIV in London. The data collection was administered via an Internet survey in order to (1) reach a wider range of potential participants and (2) protect the anonymity of the participants due to the sensitive nature of the questions being asked. Dr Stevenson was able to conduct his research by using the Internet, which has enabled him to maximise the validity of the data collected. Furthermore, this chapter outlined the advantages and disadvantages of using the Internet to conduct research on public health issues.

References

Ahern NR (2015) Using the internet to conduct research. *Nurse Researcher* 13(2): 55–70.

Barry D (2001) Assessing culture via the internet: Methods and techniques for psychological research. *CyberPsychology and Behavior* 4(1): 17–23.

Baumgartner LM (2014) "I heard he got the package": African American men's experiences of living with HIV/AIDS. *The Qualitative Report* 19(58): 1–22.

Birnbaum M (2004) Human research and data collection via the internet. *Annual Reviews in Psychology* 55: 802–832.

Bowen A, Williams M and Horvath K (2004) Using the Internet to recruit rural MSM for HIV risk assessment: Sampling issues. *AIDS and Behavior* 8(3): 311–319.

Bowker N and Keith T (2004) Using the online medium for discursive research about people with disabilities. *Social Science Computer Review* 22(2): 228–241.

Côté J, Godin G, Ramirez-Garcia P, Rouleau G, Bourbonnais A, Guéhéneuc YG, Tremblay C and Otis J (2015) Virtual intervention to support self-management of antiretroviral therapy among people living with HIV. *Journal of Medical Internet Research* 17(1): e6.

Daley EM, McDermott RJ, Brown KRM and Kittleson MJ. (2003) Conducting web based survey research: A lesson in internet designs. *American Journal of Health Behavior* 27(2): 116–124.

Duffy M (2000) The internet as a research and dissemination resource. *Health Promotion International* 15(4): 349–353.

Eaton J and Struthers CW (2002) Using the internet for organizational research: A study of cynicism in the workplace. *CyberPsychology and Behavior* 5(4): 305–313.

Eysenbach G and Till JE (2001) Ethical issues in qualitative research on internet communities. *British Medical Journal* 323: 1103–1105.

Fitzpatrick JJ and Montgomery KS (2004) *Internet for Nursing Research: A Guide to Strategies, Skills, and Resources*. Springer.

Gosling SD and Mason W (2015) Internet research in psychology. *Annual Review of Psychology* 66: 877–902.

Göritz AS (2004) Recruitment for online access panels. *International Journal of Market Research* 46(4): 411–425.

Granello DH and Wheaton JE (2002) Using web-based surveys to conduct counselling research. Report No. CG032675. ERIC Documentation Reproduction Service No. ED481144.

Guest G, Bunce A and Johnson L (2006) How many interviews are enough? An experiment with data saturation and variability. *Field Methods* 18(1): 59–82.

Hewson C (2003) Internet Research Methods. A Practical Guide for the Social and Behavioral Sciences (e-book). New Technologies for Social Research. London: SAGE.

Highton S and Finn MD (2015). HIV positive men as fathers: Accounts of displacement, ir/responsibility and paternal emergence. *Health: An Interdisciplinary Journal for the Social Study of Health, Illness and Medicine* 20(3): 291–307.

Im E and Chee W (2004) Issues in Internet survey research among cancer patients. *Cancer Nursing* 27(1): 34–44.

Kako PM, Stevens PE, Mkandawire-Valhmu L, Kibicho J, Karani AK and Dressel A (2013) Missed opportunities for early HIV diagnosis: Critical insights from stories of Kenyan women living with HIV. *International Journal of Health Promotion and Education* 51(5). doi:10.1080/14635240.2012.750070.

Kraut R, Olson J, Banaji M, Bruckman A, Cohen J and Couper M (2004) Psychological research online: Report of Board of Scientific Affairs' Advisory Group on the Conduct of Research on the Internet. *The American Psychologist* 59(2): 105–117.

Magnani R, Sabin K, Saidel T and Heckathorn D (2005) Review of sampling hard-to-reach and hidden populations for HIV surveillance. *AIDS* 19: S67–S72.

Malave S, Ramakrishna J, Heylen E, Bharat S and Ekstrand ML (2014) Differences in testing, stigma, and perceived consequences of stigmatization among heterosexual men and women living with HIV in Bengaluru, India. *AIDS Care* 26(3): 396–403.

Meyerson P and Tryon WW (2003) Validating internet research: A test of the psychometric equivalence of internet and in-person samples. *Behavioral Research Methods Instrument & Computers* 35(4): 614–620.

O'Brien KK, Solomon P, Worthington C, Ibáñez-Carrasco F, Baxter L and Nixon S (2014) Considerations for conducting web-based survey research with people living with human immunodeficiency virus using a community-based participatory approach. *Journal of Medical Internet Research* 16(3): e81.

Pittenger D (2003) Internet research: An opportunity to revisit classic ethical problems in behavior research. *Ethics and Behavior* 13(1): 45–60.

Research Unit in Behavioral and Social Issues, Gregorios HIV/AIDS Clinic, Larnaca Hospital, Cyprus Family Planning Association, KENTHEA, Cultural and Scientific Research Society (CRS) (2005). The Needs of People Living with HIV. Available online at: www.rubsi.org/en/publications/needs-people-aids

Rhodes SD, Bowie DA and Hergenrather KC (2003) Collecting behavioural data using the world wide web: Considerations for researchers. *Journal of Epidemiology and Community Health* 57(1): 68–73.

Ritter RS, Preston JL and Hernandez I (2014) Happy Tweets: Christians are happier, more socially connected and less analytical than atheists on Twitter. *Social Psychological and Personality Science* 5: 243–249.

Roos M (2002) Methods of Internet data collection and implications for recruiting respondents. *Statistical Journal of the United Nations* 19(3): 175–196.

Stewart S (2003) Casting the net: Using the internet for survey research. *British Journal of Midwifery* 11(9): 543–546.

Strickland OL, Moloney MF, Dietrich AS, Myerburg S, Cotsonis GA and Johnson RV (2003) Measurement issues related to data collection on the worldwide web. *Advances in Nursing Science* 26(4): 246–256.

Wilson R (2003) The internet makes gathering data quick, easy and cheap. *Nursing Standard* 18(6): 20.

Wolf M, Theis F and Kordy H (2013) Language use in eating disorder blogs: Psychological implications of social online activity. *Journal of Language Social Psychology* 32: 212–226.

8 Secondary data research

Mental illness

Abstract

Dr Janet Gordon is a psychiatrist and is faced with a challenge from a psychiatric patient's relative who believes that mental hospitals are like prisons, whose aim is to keep patients hidden from the public. The relative also argues that the mental hospital where Dr Gordon is practising has always been a prison-like place for the mentally ill. Dr Gordon is interested in examining the hospital's archives in order to understand how the procedures of controlling the patients have changed over the years.

Studying mental illness is the main focus of this chapter, which discusses mental hospitals as stigmatising social contexts. To further investigate and understand the controlling nature of mental hospitals, this chapter explores the use of data archives to understand changing procedures and practices.

Learning objectives:

- Describe the main research findings from studies on the experience of mental illness and psychiatric hospitalisation.
- Explain what secondary analysis of quantitative data sources is, and also explain the role of data archives in secondary analysis.
- Describe the main methodological issues associated with secondary analysis, as well as the ethical considerations in secondary analysis.
- Outline the advantages and disadvantages of using data archives for secondary analysis of quantitative data sources.

Scenario

Dr Janet Gordon is a psychiatrist and is interested in research. She conducted both quantitative and qualitative research for her PhD studies and would like to carry on with examining patients' satisfaction with psychiatric services; however, she never had the chance to pursue it. Recently, she was faced with a challenge from a psychiatric patient's relative who believed that mental hospitals were like prisons, which aimed to keep patients hidden from the public. The relative also argued that the mental hospital Janet was now practising at had always been a prison-like place for the mentally ill. The relative highlighted that healthcare professionals have been hostile towards patients and that they mainly enforce controlling rules. As the relative was very adamant, Janet was motivated to explore these claims through research.

Janet thought to conduct in-depth qualitative interviews with the healthcare professionals and formulated her research question. That is, what is the relationship between healthcare professionals and patients? Janet wanted to do this properly, so she prepared a detailed research proposal for the hospital's management to review and applied for the required ethics review. Janet conducted six interviews to begin with; she analysed them and checked for initial data saturation. She was close to achieving saturation and was thinking of continuing with her interviews. However, her findings so far indicated something striking. That is, the healthcare professionals she interviewed told her that the patients were well treated, they had free time and they were involved in various activities, and that, although there were some difficult patients, they were all treated with respect and dignity. These findings were inconsistent with what the relative had told her previously.

There were two possibilities that might account for this. First, the relative was exaggerating because something or someone at the hospital had annoyed him or her. Second, Janet's participants were not telling her the truth. Janet checked the methodology literature once again and was reminded of the Hawthorne effect, whereby research participants alter their behaviour or attitudes when they know they are being studied. Therefore, Janet was asking her participants about an issue they were directly involved with, which they, perhaps, did not want to acknowledge or did not want to take personal responsibility for. Interestingly, when she discussed her preliminary findings with a researcher outside the hospital, the researcher asked her "What is the daily schedule for patients? Are there any written rules about the patients' behaviour?"

Discuss

- How could Janet address these questions?
- Could Janet answer these questions by carrying on with her qualitative research?
- Are there any other research methods which might be more helpful?

Janet did not know the answers to these questions because she was a visiting scientist at the hospital; however, she was motivated to further investigate the matter. She considered changing her research methodology to collating, coding and analysing data archives and secondary data from the hospital. Before embarking on this new endeavour, Janet reviewed the literature to see whether other studies had identified whether mental hospitals' rules and measures were indeed controlling.

Mental illness, psychiatric hospitalisation and stigma

According to qualitative studies, confinement to a mental hospital appears to be harmful for people with severe mental illness due to the lack of focus on the patients' needs, the deficiency of the services offered, and the experiences of oppression and coercion (Kaite *et al.*, 2015; McKay, 2010; Schön, 2009; Schön, 2013). Within psychiatric mental health hospitals, several coercive measures are required, such as mechanical restraints, especially in cases where the patient is a danger to him/herself and to others (Lanthén *et al.*, 2015). Qualitative studies (Chien *et al.*, 2005) on the lived experience of mechanical restraints reveal feelings of fear, humiliation or punishment. In addition, other studies (Bonner *et al.*, 2002; Fish *et al.*, 2005; Wynn, 2004), have found that patients perceived mechanical restraint as a means of reliving traumatic memories. Of course, when sufficient information and support were provided by staff as to the use of mechanical restraints, neutral reactions occurred (Chien *et al.*, 2005).

Furthermore, a longitudinal study conducted by Link *et al.* (2008) on stigma and coercion in an outpatient setting revealed that coercion led to more perceived stigma and lower levels of quality of life and self-esteem. In line with the aforementioned study are studies by Evans-Lacko (2012) and Schomerus *et al.* (2012), which underlined that coercion increases vulnerability to self-stigma and public stigma. Moreover, a qualitative study (Runte-Geidel *et al.*, 2014) in Spain aimed to explore the opinions of inmates and staff of mental psychiatric hospitals and prisons in relation to the use of coercive measures for clinical reasons through four focus groups. Forced medication was identified as the most commonly used coercive measure in both institutions. Inmates objected to this due to the lack of information about their illness and the required medication.

It is also interesting to note that international literature (Verhaeghe *et al.*, 2008) makes a distinction between the length and type of duration of psychiatric hospitalisation with stigma experiences. In particular, Verhaeghe *et al.* (2008) conducted a survey on 378 clients of 42 wards from 8 psychiatric hospitals in an effort to investigate whether or not part-time hospitalisation in psychiatric hospitals is associated with less experience of stigma compared with full-time hospitalisation. The results showed that part-time clients who had no previous experience of full-time hospitalisation reported less social rejection than clients who received full-time hospitalisation. In contrast, there are other studies (Mazor and Doron, 2011) that highlight the need for and importance of the contribution of confinement in a psychiatric mental hospital, especially in the relapse period and when psychotic symptoms are active.

Discuss

- How could this information help Janet with her study?

Janet can see now that the hospitalisation of mental patients might be a controlling and stigmatising experience for the patients, and she can better appreciate the complaints she received earlier from the patient's relative. She continues by delving into the research and analysis of the data archives at the hospital. Janet had a clear research question. That is, is psychiatric hospitalisation controlling and stigmatising to patients? To answer this question, Janet collated secondary data, such as previous and existing procedures, previous and existing treatment protocols, patient files, patient satisfaction surveys, healthcare satisfaction surveys, and registered patients' and relatives' complaints.

Definition of secondary and archive data

Secondary analysis is a form of analysis of an existing dataset collected and analysed for a different purpose than the one that the data were initially collected for (Dale *et al.*, 2008; Vartanian, 2010). In other words, it is the reanalysis of data collected by another researcher or organisation. It is widely used for conducting international comparative studies, as well as studies that seek to cover many countries and/or trends over time (Hakim, 1987). Secondary data derive, among other sources, from surveys and census data collected by the government, surveys conducted by academics, journal supplements and authors' websites (Dale *et al.*, 2008). McCaston (2005) presented six main sources of secondary data:

1 Official statistics gathered by various agencies and departments for the purpose of understanding trends and forming policy-making decisions
2 Technical reports including research findings that are prepared to inform interested parties, such as departments, governments, institutions and so forth
3 Scholarly journals, which make available research articles
4 Literature review articles, which can also be useful resources because they usually list publications specific to topics
5 Trade journals that have articles relevant to specific fields
6 Reference books such as handbooks, manuals and dictionaries

Additionally, secondary data are available from government offices, institutions, libraries, international organisations and so on. Andersen *et al.* (2011) highlighted the importance of distinguishing between archive data and secondary data. While secondary data are data collected for specific purposes, archive data refer to letters, newspaper articles and organisational records.

Data archives can also be storehouses of digitised data, used for various functions such as obtaining data, assessing suitability for release, checking the data, and adding the necessary data description and documentation and preserving the data for future use. Data can be downloaded from websites in forms readable by SPSS or NVivo, or in some cases, data would be available in an open access format that would require ethics approval for reanalysing, and this would take more time than estimated or even need more money in order to obtain access to specific CDs on which the data are available (Seale, 2012).

Researchers can search for a dataset in various ways, including searching through a local archive that can be found through CESSDA (for Europe) (http://cessda.net/), the IFDO website (http://ifdo.org/wordpress/) or the UK Survey

Question Bank (http://surveynet.ac.uk/sqb/). In addition, a researcher can search through major social survey organisations. If a researcher wishes to use a dataset from another country and this is restricted to users within the country of origin, s/he can follow access procedures or access CESSDA, which enables researchers to explore a variety of data published by major European national archives. A researcher can also conduct a literature review in order to locate the availability of a data source and explore other information sources (mainly web-based).

Before using specific data surveys for reanalysis, one needs to check first whether the specific survey contains relevant information. Usually, information is located on the archive's website, and in many cases there is the option of downloading data and immediately starting the analysis after downloading the relevant files (Seale, 2012). There is also the option of accessing qualitative data archives, which could be found at the UK ESDS Qualidata website (www.esds.ac.uk/qualidata/about/introduction.asp), the Finnish Social Science Data Archive (www.fsd.uta.fi/en/) and the Life-Course Archive in Germany (www.qualitative-research.net/index.php/fqs).

Corti and Thompson (2004) list six main uses of qualitative data that could be applied to statistical data:

- Description
- Comparative research, restudy or follow up
- Reanalysis or secondary analysis
- Research design and methodological advancement (reviewing existing semi-structured questionnaires in order to develop a semi-structured guide based on the literature)
- Verification – if a study makes important claims, other researchers can examine its original data to assess the evidence in support of those claims
- Teaching and learning (Corti and Thompson, 2004, cited in Seale, 2016: 307)

Qualitative secondary analysis involves the reuse of pre-existing qualitative data derived from previous research studies, which include semi-structured interviews, responses to open-ended questions in questionnaires, and filled notes and research diaries (Heaton, 2008). Qualitative secondary analysis is not a documentary analysis or meta-analysis. Documentary analysis works with naturalistic materials (e.g. autobiographies, personal diaries and photographs). Meta-analysis and systematic reviews are methods that require the researcher to merely return to the findings of previous studies and not revisit or rework the data (Heaton, 2008). However, there are some limitations in using these qualitative data archives due to the fact that they are mainly available in older study forms and you may need to travel to consult the original documentation, or view and listen to videotapes or audiotapes (Seale, 2016).

Janet is quite confident now that using secondary and archive data can help her to better gauge the former and existing situation at the hospital and to better understand the experiences of her patients, without asking them to express their opinions. Though the secondary data was not collected for research purposes, it will give Janet the opportunity to develop an overall picture and address her research question about the controlling and stigmatising nature of psychiatric hospitals. Since she is using different types of secondary data, Janet will be able to triangulate her findings. Triangulation would show that any conclusions arrived at are more valid and substantial.

> **Discuss**
>
> - How could Janet proceed with secondary data research?
> - Could Janet start with a research question or would it be better to look at the data first?

Approaches to analysing existing data

The first approach used in analysing existing data refers to an a priori hypothesis or question that researchers have in mind and that leads them to search for suitable datasets to address this question, and is known as *the research question-driven approach (*Cheng and Philips, 2014). The second approach used is known as the *data-driven approach*, in which researchers first have a look at the dataset and then decide what questions can be answered through it. Based on Cheng and Philips' explanation, Janet's approach is research question driven in the sense that she formulated a research question first and she will then analyse the secondary data. However, Janet was inspired by comments made by the relative of one of her mental patients. This trigger could be viewed as a type of data, which laid the ground for Janet's research. This trigger or data is reminiscent of "shadow data" (Morse, 2000), which refers to information that does not come directly from the research participants but rather, from other people who know the research participants.

Cheng and Philips carried on arguing that, in practice, the aforementioned approaches were often used simultaneously and in repetition. Researchers start with a general idea about the question or hypothesis and then look for available datasets, which contain the variables needed to address the research questions of interest. In the event that they do not find datasets that include all the necessary variables in order to address their research question, they often alter the research question(s) or the analysis based on the available data (Cheng and Philips, 2014).

Moreover, Hakim (1987) refers to three other approaches of conducting secondary analysis: the use of a single dataset in order to replicate the original results or to address completely different questions; the use of a single dataset extended by the addition of data from other sources; and the use of multiple datasets in order to assess findings on a topic, to ascertain results that are robust enough not to depend heavily on the particular procedures used in any individual study or its location in time, and to study trends and changes over a long period of time and carry out area-based research (cross-national comparative studies).

There are three additional ways of undertaking secondary analysis: formal data sharing, where the researcher can access datasets available in public or institutional archives and reuse them in secondary research (reuse data independently collected by others); informal data sharing, where primary researchers may share their data with others who were not involved in the original research and, thus, may lead or participate in the secondary analysis research team (alternatively, two or more primary researchers might pool their own datasets, which they collected separately, and work with other independent researchers in carrying out secondary data analysis); and reusing their own self-collected data in order to investigate new or additional questions to those explored in the primary research or to verify their previous findings. The last can be done by teaming up and combining respective datasets (an element of informal data sharing, but researchers who were involved in one or more of the primary studies are involved in the secondary analysis), or a sole researcher or team of primary researchers can reuse data that they themselves previously collected for secondary research purposes (without involving any other independent researchers) (Heaton, 2008).

Discuss

- Having finalised her research question, how could Janet proceed with secondary data research?
- Having found her dataset, how could Janet now proceed with her analysis?
- Could her prior experience in qualitative and quantitative research be of any help?

Process of conducting and analysing secondary and archive data

Andersen *et al.* (2011: 58–72) presented a step-by-step guide for designing and conducting secondary data research. Step 1 is the identification of appropriate secondary data to meet the research purpose or adequately address the research question. There are many actions that need to be considered under this step. That is, a researcher first needs to make sure that there is an available dataset. Furthermore, a researcher should clarify the group of people under study. This is because the study of different groups may require different datasets. Finally, the researcher needs to make sure that the identified data is accessible. Step 2 is to create a personalised dataset. This means organising the project and having a clear course of action from taking notes to filing. Andersen *et al.* went on to explain that reading the work of others who have used the same dataset can inform a researcher more precisely as to how to proceed. A critical action to undertake at this point is the creation of a guide for coding, as well as a codebook.

In Step 3, a researcher should proceed more deeply into the analysis and create variables. This is necessary in cases where datasets have qualitative information, which needs to be quantified and turned into variables. Andersen *et al.* (2011) explained that the final step involves statistical considerations. That is, the researchers need to consider missing data and sampling and be mindful of what might be the outcome from using very large samples. The problem with very large samples is that they may show statistically significant relationships between unimportant variables.

Cheng and Philips (2014) outlined a similar process. First, researchers should document everything by creating an abridged codebook describing the original and recoded variables of interest. Afterwards, researchers must transfer all potential data of interest to a new file, using electronic codebooks (ECBS) and not altering the original data file. The second step refers to addressing missing data by identifying missing values in a software program and, when possible, using knowledge of skip patterns to recode missing data as meaningful values and selecting a method for handling missing data (e.g. multiple imputation, full information maximum likelihood [FIML]). Step 3 includes the recoding of variables and, especially, the effort to reverse code negatively worded items in the case of creating scale scores, dummy code dichotomous variables into values of 0,1 (e.g. the original dataset may use values of 1,2), and recode other categorical variables (e.g. dummy or effect coding). It may also be necessary to combine separate but like variables and recode variables so that all the responses will be based on the same units. Step 4 refers to the creation of new variables, since the researcher may need to recreate composite variables if there is a disagreement with the original conceptualisation. Lastly, in the case of psychometric work, the researcher should create scores from individual items using factor analysis or item response theory and, to avoid potentially biased variance estimates, the researcher should either incorporate measurement models directly into the analysis or output "plausible values" (Cheng and Philips, 2014).

However, before beginning analysis there are six questions (Dale *et al.*, 1988) that the researcher must ask:

1 What was the purpose of the original study and what conceptual framework informed it?
2 What information has been collected and is it on subjects relevant to the concerns of the secondary analyst and in the form needed?
3 How was the sample drawn up and what biases in responders and non-responders were evident?
4 What sort of agency collected the data and how adequate were their procedures for ensuring its quality?
5 Which population does the survey represent?
6 When was the data collected, and is it still relevant to the circumstances the secondary analyst wishes to investigate? (Dale *et al.*, 1988, cited in Seale, 2016: 309)

As far as the analysis is concerned, depending on the research question set, the researcher should identify the appropriate statistical analysis, select a software package in which to implement analysis and account for complex sampling (e.g. SPSSS, or R or SASS). Afterwards, the researcher must examine unweighted descriptive statistics in order to identify coding errors and determine the adequacy of sample size, as well as identify weights to make sure that missing weights are set to 0. Further, the researcher must identify a variance estimation method as well as corresponding variables, conduct diagnostic analyses (identify outliers, non-normality, etc.) and, finally, conduct primary analysis and interpret the results.

The researcher should be extremely cautious with longitudinal studies, in which the assessment methods and the coding methods for key variables can change over time. In this case, the researcher should conduct a thorough examination of the survey questionnaires and codebooks to ensure that each variable in the combined dataset has a uniform interpretation throughout the study. In order to accomplish this, s/he might have to create separate uniform variables that are constructed differently as well as over several points in time throughout the study (e.g. the crosswalks to convert diagnostic categories between DSM-III, DSM-IV and DSM-5) (Cheng and Philips, 2014).

In addition, several population-based surveys, especially those focused on assessing the prevalence of relatively uncommon conditions such as schizophrenia, employ multi-stage sampling strategies to enrich the sample. In this case, the dataset usually includes design variables for each case that are needed to adjust the analysis of interest (e.g. prevalence of a condition, odds, ratios, mean differences, etc.). Thus, researchers should be extremely careful about the design variables used in the original study and should apply these variables appropriately in their own analyses in order to generate less biased estimates (Cheng and Philips, 2014).

What is very important for researchers of secondary data to always bear in mind is to have a clear and detailed description of the process they are using, the variables they are creating, the codes they using and the rationale for this coding. This information would make their study more scientific in the sense that it would be replicable: a major criterion for a scientific study. Also, the detailed description can serve as a framework for making sense of any differences between other secondary data studies that used the same datasets.

In secondary research, qualitative data can be analysed, too. More specifically, Heaton (2008) presented the following types of qualitative secondary data analysis:

1 Supplementary analysis: an in-depth analysis of an emergent issue or aspect of the data that had not been addressed or had been partially addressed in the primary study
2 Supra analysis: aims and focus of the secondary study transcend those of the original research
3 Reanalysis: data are re-examined to confirm and validate findings of a primary study
4 Amplified analysis: two or more qualitative datasets might be compared or combined for secondary analysis
5 Assorted analysis: reuse of existing qualitative data carried out alongside the collection and analysis of primary qualitative data for the same study, or a mix of naturalistic and non-naturalistic data

Janet realises that secondary data research is not as difficult as she initially thought. This is due to her experience with both quantitative and qualitative research. Drawing from her prior experience, she identified many similarities between secondary data research and quantitative/qualitative methodology. First, having a clear research question before commencing with data collection is fundamental. Second, similarly to conducting quantitative/qualitative research, she has to personalise her project and develop a good plan as well as a clear study design. Third, prior knowledge of statistical analysis is important for analysing secondary quantitative data. Fourth, coding and codebooks are the basis for having a robust analysis of the qualitative data that can potentially derive from secondary and archival data. Another important aspect in the process that Janet is now aware of is the role of exploring the basic literature. This helped Janet understand the broader issue, that is, the control of mental patients in mental hospitals, and formulate a specific and clear research question. The basic literature works as a guide through the following steps and the overall organisation of the study.

Discuss

- Are there any ethical issues in secondary data research that Janet could be aware of?

Ethics in secondary data research

The researchers who conducted the primary analysis have already obtained all the ethical approvals required and have followed all the ethical principles. However, when conducting secondary analysis, researchers must still preserve confidentiality. This means that there might be cases in which the researchers may not be able to obtain as much detailed data as they need. Further, they must respect professional conduct by maintaining awareness of the necessary law and legislation, reporting the limitations of their data and method, and respecting privacy and maintaining the confidentiality of data (Alasuutari *et al.*, 2008).

In relation to qualitative secondary data analysis, researchers also need to deal with issues of confidentiality, anonymity and legal issues, such as copyright and data protection. In the UK, specific guidelines have been developed by the ESDS Qualidata (www.ukdataservice.ac.uk/manage-data/legal-ethical) and the Economic and Social Research Council (ESRC) (www.esrc.ac.uk/funding/guidance-for-applicants/research-ethics/). In addition, researchers should use data solely for statistical purposes related to their project and destroy them afterwards and/or safeguard data by storing them in a safe place. Data should also be used in an appropriate way, and this requires reading all the relevant documentation so that the researcher will know how the information was collected and compiled and what biases and inaccuracies may be found in the data (Alasuutari *et al.*, 2008).

Several ethical issues in relation to sampling methods are also raised, particularly in the case of survey samples, where the researcher must ensure that information on sampling design informs the analysis. Further, issues concerning non-response might also be revealed. Non-respondents differ from respondents, with obvious consequences for the validity of the results of any analysis, while the manner in which the non-responses are distributed is of ethical concern. Moreover, if the dataset is very detailed and contains personal information, the data should be made available under licence, whereby the user must agree to a set of conditions designed to ensure the confidentiality of the data. If researchers require more detailed data (e.g. to include information on locality, or if more datasets are produced by linking administrative records), tighter controls should be applied (Alasuutari *et al.*, 2008).

Janet realises that anonymity is not guaranteed in the case of her study, as she is conducting secondary data research in a specific mental hospital, which might lead to presenting data through which individuals may be identified. This raises concerns for both Janet and the hospital's management. To deal with the potential risk of disclosing personal data, Janet decides to expand her research to include other mental hospitals in the region.

Advantages and disadvantages of secondary data analysis

Janet now has a clear research question and a plan for how to proceed. She knows that secondary and archival data research have certain advantages and disadvantages. However, she is confident that the advantages in her case outweigh the disadvantages because her initial primary research did not elicit reliable data regarding the controlling nature of mental hospitals.

The main advantage of using secondary data analysis relates to the fact that this methodology saves time and money, since it offers the researcher the opportunity to access international and cross-historical data that would otherwise take several years and a significant amount of funding to compile (Hakim, 1987; Bryman and Tevin, 2005; Cheng and Phillips, 2014; Punch, 2005). This makes it a preferable choice of analysis for students (Punch, 2005). The second major advantage is that it offers high-quality data, since most of the datasets accessed have used large and representative samples, thus having greater external validity, as well as the likelihood that the former studies used oversampling of low-prevalence groups and behaviours, which allows increased statistical precision (Punch, 2005). Additionally, the included datasets often contain numerous variables, and secondary data analysis offers the opportunity for longitudinal analysis as well as subgroup analysis (e.g. in the case of General Social Survey [GSS]), where larger samples are included in the data source and offer the opportunity to study what can often be quite sizeable subgroups. Furthermore, the opportunity for cross-cultural analysis can also be provided by facilitating the use of common core questions in national surveys and in various surveys conducted in other countries (Bryman and Teevan, 2005). Survey micro data used as the basis for international comparative studies can lead to recoding and reclassification that would establish comparability between the datasets used (Hakim, 1987).

In addition, secondary data analysis provides the opportunity for reanalysis, which could result in new interpretations of the data. For example, one secondary analyst may look at relationships between variables that had not been predicted by the primary researchers, prompting a reconsideration of the relevance of the data as well as offering the prospect of a rather distinct interpretation of the data, which are continuously emerging in disciplines such as statistics and even within the social sciences themselves (Bryman and Teevan, 2005). Finally, Long-Sutehall *et al.* (2010) explained that using secondary and archival data is particularly useful when the topics under study are sensitive or when the study populations are not easily accessible. More researchers use secondary and archival data nowadays, as modern technology has made the study of such data widely available (Johnston, 2014).

However, there are several disadvantages to secondary analysis, such as

- The researchers undertaking secondary analysis are not those who conducted the primary data collection and, as a consequence, they have a more distant relationship to the data and a period of familiarisation with the data must be considered as essential (Cheng and Phillips, 2014)
- The complexity of the data can lead to ecological fallacy, the error of assuming that inferences about individuals can be made from aggregate data (Bryman and Teevan, 2008)
- Key variables may be absent, since some key variables might not be available for analysis or data might not have been collected from all the population subgroups of interest or from all the geographic regions of interest (Cheng and Philips, 2014)

In addition, key variables might be missing in order to preserve the anonymity and confidentiality of the participants in primary research: variables such as zip codes, the names of the primary sampling units, and so on, which are essential for the intended analysis (Cheng and Philips, 2014).

Moreover, there may be some problems in relation to the validity and reliability of the data collected using secondary sources as far as the variety of the information collected is concerned (e.g. information obtained from a census is more likely to be valid and reliable than information obtained from personal diaries). Personal bias can also occur when the researcher uses information from personal diaries, newspapers and magazines, since those authors are likely to exhibit less thoroughness and objectivity in contrast to research reports (Kumar, 2005). Lastly, there may be problems with thc availablc format of the data, since in some cases the data might not be available in the required format. For example, a researcher may want to analyse age in specific categories (e.g. 25–35, 36–45 and so on) but in the source data, age may be categorised differently (e.g. 25–30, 31–35 and so on) (Kumar, 2005).

Similarly, in relation to qualitative secondary analysis there are some issues raised, such as the problem of data fit (whether data collected for one [primary] purpose can be reused for another [secondary] purpose); the problem of not having been there: trying to interpret data that were not collected by the researcher (interpretation of qualitative data from archives, secondary analysis of informally shared data and primary analysis of data collected by teams in which different researchers carry out interviews and jointly analyse them); and the problem of verification: whether the results of qualitative research can or should be verified in the same way as studies using statistical methods (thus, methods have been established to measure the "trustworthiness" and authenticity of the qualitative data) (Heaton, 2008). The best known is that established by Lincoln and Guba (1985), who identified that researchers need to establish credibility: confidence in the "truth" of the findings; transferability: that findings can be applied in other contexts; dependability: to show that the findings are consistent and could be repeated; and confirmability: the extent to which the findings of the study are shaped by the respondents and not researcher bias, motivation or interest.

Conclusion

In this chapter, Janet tried to understand the relationship between healthcare professionals and psychiatric patients by interviewing the former. However, she soon discovered that her research participants were not telling her the truth, possibly because they did not want to expose themselves. Due to the sensitivity of the issue and the methodological challenges, Janet chose secondary data analysis as a method of examining the hospital's archives and, thus, improving the circumstances of psychiatric patients. Secondary data analysis is a useful method for exploring sensitive issues and generating conclusions that cannot easily be reached through other methods, such as interviews or questionnaires.

References

Alasuutari P, Bickman L and Brannen J (2008). *The SAGE Handbook of Social Research Methods*. London: SAGE.

Andersen JP, Prause J and Silver RC (2011) A step-by-step guide to using secondary data for psychological research. *Social and Personality Psychology Compass* 5(1): 56–75.

Bonner G, Lowe T, Rawcliffe D and Wellman, N (2002) Trauma for all: A pilot study of the subjective experience of physical restraint for mental health inpatients and staff in the UK. *Journal of Psychiatric and Mental Health Nursing* 9(4): 465–473.

Bryman A and Teevan JJ (2005) *Social Research Methods*. New York: Oxford University Press.

Cessda Consortium of European Social Science Data Archives (n.d.) Available online at: http://cessda.net/. Accessed 12 December 2015.

Cheng HG and Phillips MR (2014) Secondary analysis of existing data: Opportunities and implementation. *Shanghai Archives of Psychiatry* 26(6): 371.

Chien W-T, Chan CWH, Lam L-W and Kam CW (2005) Psychiatric inpatients' perceptions of positive and negative aspects of physical restraint. *Patient Education and Counselling* 59(1): 80–86.

Dale A, Wathan J and Higgins V (2008) Secondary analysis of quantitative data sources. In: Alasuutari P, Bickman L and Brannen J (eds) *The Sage Handbook of Social Research Methods*. London: SAGE, pp. 520–535.

Economic and Social Research Council (ESRC) (n.d.) Available online at: www.esrc.ac.uk/funding/guidance-for-applicants/research-ethics/. Accessed 29 July 2016.

Evans-Lacko S, Henderson C and Thornicroft G (2013) Public knowledge, attitudes and behaviour regarding people with mental illness in England 2009–2012. *The British Journal of Psychiatry* 202(s55): s51–s57.

ESDS Qualidata website (n.d.) Available online at: www.esds.ac.uk/qualidata/about/introduction.asp. Accessed 29 July 2016.

Finnish Social Science Data Archive (n.d.) Available online at: www.fsd.uta.fi/en/. Accessed 29 July 2916.

Fish R and Culshaw E (2005) The last resort? Staff and client perspectives on physical intervention. *Journal of Intellectual Disabilities* 9(2): 93–107.

Forum Qualitative Social Research (n.d.) Available online at: www.qualitative-research.net/index.php/fqs. Accessed 29 July 2016.

Hakim C (1987) *Research Design. Strategies and Choices in the Design of Social Research*. London: Routledge.

Heaton J (2008) Secondary analysis of qualitative data: An overview. *Historical Social Research/Historische Sozialforschung* 33(3): 33–45.

International Federation of Data Organizations for Social Sciences (IFDO, n.d.) Available online at: http://ifdo.org/wordpress/. Accessed 12 December 2015.

Johnston M (2014) Secondary data analysis: A method of which the time has come. *Qualitative and Quantitative Research Methods in Libraries* 3: 619–626.

Kaite C (2015) A phenomenological exploration of the lived experience of mentally ill patients in Cyprus. (Doctoral dissertation, Cyprus University of Technology, 2015).

Koziol N and Arthur A (n.d.) *An Introduction to Secondary Data Analysis* [PowerPoint slides]. Children Youth Families and School Nebraska Centre for Research Online. Available online at: http://r2ed.unl.edu/presentations/2011/RMS/120911_Koziol/120911_Koziol.pdf. Accessed 29 July 2016.

Kumar, R. (2005). *Research Methodology: A Step by Step Guide for Beginners*. London: Thousand Oaks.

Lanthén K, Rask M and Sunnqvist C (2015) Psychiatric patients' experiences with mechanical restraints: An interview study. *Psychiatry Journal* 2015: 748392.

Lincoln YS and Guba EG (1985) *Naturalistic Inquiry*. Newbury Park: SAGE.

Link B, Castille DM and Stuber J (2008) Stigma and coercion in the context of outpatient treatment for people with mental illnesses. *Social Science & Medicine* 67(3): 409–419.

Long-Sutehall T (2010) Secondary analysis of qualitative data: A valuable method for exploring sensitive issues with an elusive population? *Journal of Research in Nursing* 16(4): 335–344.

McCaston MK (2005) Tips for collecting, reviewing, and analyzing secondary data. Updated from McCaston 1998. Partnership and Household Livelihood Security Unit. Atlanta, GA: CARE.

McKay EA (2010) Rip that book up, I've changed: Unveiling the experiences of women living with and surviving enduring mental illness. *British Journal of Occupational Therapy* 73(3): 96–105.

Mazor U and Doron I (2011) The meaning of community rehabilitation for schizophrenia patients in Israel. *Community Mental Health Journal* 47(3): 351–360.

Morse JM (2000) Determining sample size. *Qualitative Health Research* 10(1): 3–5.

Punch KF (2005) *Introduction to Social Research: Quantitative and Qualitative Approaches*. London: SAGE.

Ranjit K (2005) *Research Methodology: A Step-by-Step Guide for Beginners*. London: Thousand Oaks.

Republic of Cyprus, Statistical Service (n.d.) Available online at: www.mof.gov.cy/mof/cystat/statistics.nsf/index_en/index_en?OpenDocument. Accessed 12 December 2015.

Runte-Geidel A, Girela E, López A, Ruiz F and Torres-González F (2014) Study of coercive measures in prisons and secure psychiatric hospitals: The views of inmates and caregivers. *Revista española de sanidad penitenciaria* 16(1): 3.

Schomerus G, Schwahn C, Holzinger A, Corrigan PW, Grabe HJ, Carta MG and Angermeyer MC (2012) Evolution of public attitudes about mental illness: A systematic review and meta-analysis. *Acta Psychiatrica Scandinavica* 125(6): 440–452.

Schön UK (2013) Recovery in involuntary psychiatric care: Is there a gender difference? *Journal of Mental Health* 22(5): 420–427.

Schön UK (2009) How men and women in recovery give meaning to severe mental illness. *Journal of Mental Health* 18(5): 433–440.

Seale C (2012) *Researching Society and Culture* (3rd ed.). London: SAGE.

Survey Question bank (n.d.) Available online at: http://surveynet.ac.uk/sqb/. Accessed 29 July 2016.

Verhaeghe M, Bracke P and Christiaens W (2008) Part-time hospitalisation and stigma experiences: A study in contemporary psychiatric hospitals. *BMC Health Services Research* 8(1): 125.

Wynn R (2004) Psychiatric inpatients' experiences with restraint. *Journal of Forensic Psychiatry and Psychology* 15(1): 124–144.

9 Combining quantitative and qualitative research methods

Alzheimer's disease

Abstract

Dr James White treats older patients living with Alzheimer's disease and is interested in recording the number of changes in his patients' lives, as well as understanding what it means to live with Alzheimer's disease. Dr White thinks that a combination of quantitative and qualitative research methods will provide him with a more holistic picture of his patients' experiences.

This chapter explores the literature in the epidemiology of living with Alzheimer's disease and focuses on the importance of combining quantitative and qualitative research methods to understand a phenomenon more holistically, as well as on the triangulation of data deriving from different research methodologies.

Learning objectives:

- Explore the literature on the epidemiology of living with Alzheimer's disease.
- Record the number of changes in the life of patients living with Alzheimer's disease.
- Explore the lived experience of Alzheimer's disease.
- Justify the need for using mixed methods for understanding the phenomenon more holistically, as well as the triangulation of data deriving from different methodologies.

Scenario

Dr James White treats older patients living with Alzheimer's disease. His patients and their relatives tell him many stories about the difficulties and challenges they face on account of the disease and that Alzheimer's disease is one of the worst conditions someone could have. Some of his patients state that living with Alzheimer's disease can be worse than dealing with cancer. James wonders why this is the case and is interested in learning more about the disease so that he can better understand and support his patients. Therefore, he initially considers recording the number of changes in his patients' lives, as well as understanding what it means to live with Alzheimer's disease. James thinks that a combination of quantitative and qualitative research methods will provide him with a more holistic view of his patients' experiences. However, he is uncertain about exactly what to explore and he has not clearly identified his research question. James reviews the existing literature carefully to reshape his thoughts and refine his focus.

Definition of Alzheimer's disease

Alzheimer's disease is a neurocognitive disorder (NCD). According to the Diagnostic and Statistical Manual of Mental Disorders (DSM-5),

> The NCD category encompasses the group of disorders in which the primary clinical deficit is in cognitive function, and are acquired rather than developmental. Although cognitive deficits are present in many if not all mental disorders (e.g. schizophrenia, bipolar disorders), only disorders whose core features are cognitive are included in the NCD category. The NCDs are those in which impaired cognition has not been present since birth or very early in life, and thus represents a decline from a previously attained level of functioning.
>
> (American Psychiatric Association, 2013: 591)

Major or mild neurocognitive disorder due to Alzheimer's disease must fulfil some specific criteria, including:

- A The criteria are met for major or mild neurocognitive disorder.
- B There is insidious onset and gradual progression of impairment in one or more cognitive domains (for major neurocognitive disorder, at least two domains must be impaired).
- C Criteria are met for either probable or possible Alzheimer's disease as follows:
  - 1 Evidence of a causative Alzheimer's disease genetic mutation from family history or genetic testing.
  - 2 All three of the following are present:
    - a Clear evidence of decline in memory and learning and at least one other cognitive domain (based on detailed history or serial neuropsychological testing).
    - b Steadily progressive, gradual decline in cognition, without extended plateaus.
    - c No evidence of mixed etiology (i.e. absence of other neurodegenerative or cerebrovascular disease, or another neurological, mental or systemic disease or condition likely contributing to cognitive decline).

D The disturbance is not better explained by cerebrovascular disease, another neurodegenerative disease, the effects of a substance, or another mental, neurological or systemic disorder.

(American Psychiatric Association, 2013: 611)

It must be noted that there is a great deal of diversity of symptoms among patients; however, the most usual symptoms include a dysfunction in memory, planning or solving problems; difficulty completing familiar tasks; confusion with time or place; difficulty in understanding visual images and spatial relationships; difficulty with words in speaking or writing; the individual is unable to find things; deterioration of judgement; work or social withdrawal; mood and personality alterations, with most commonly apathy and depression and, overall, a major decline in a person's daily activities (Alzheimer's Association, 2015).

A variety of risk factors are found to be associated with the development of this disease, such as age (more common in people aged 65 or older) and the inheritance of the apolipoprotein E (APOE)-e4 gene, which is a gene responsible for a protein that transports cholesterol in the bloodstream. In addition, heredity (genetics) is considered to be a factor, especially when an individual's parent or sibling suffers from Alzheimer's disease (Loy *et al.*, 2014). People with mild cognitive impairment (MCI), an impairment in thinking and memory that is considered to be mild, are more likely to develop Alzheimer's disease than people without MCI; however, this is not considered to be an absolute factor.

Moreover, other factors that are considered to be high risk for developing Alzheimer's disease include smoking (Rusanen *et al.*, 2011), obesity (Loef and Walach, 2013), hypertension (Ninomiya *et al.*, 2011; Rönnemaa *et al.*, 2011) and cholesterol (Meng *et al.*, 2014). Lack of social education as well as cognitive engagement, and traumatic brain injury (TBI), are also considered to be risk factors. In the case of education, international literature (Stern, 2012) supports the idea that people who have years of formal education are not at a high risk of developing the disease. As far as cognitive engagement is concerned, this is mentioned as a protective factor rather than a risk factor (Di Marco *et al.*, 2014).

The epidemiology of living with Alzheimer's disease

In the USA, it is estimated that 5.1 million people aged 65 years and older will suffer from Alzheimer's disease (Hebert *et al.*, 2013). There is also a difference in gender occurrence of the disease, with two-thirds of Americans with Alzheimer's disease being women (Hebert *et al.*, 2013). Reasons for the incidence of higher prevalence among women focus on the fact that women have a higher life expectancy than men, as well as on biological or genetic variations and differences in life experiences (i.e. amount of education or occupational choices). In addition, the APOE-e4 genotype has been found to have a stronger relationship to Alzheimer's disease in women than in men (Altmann *et al.*, 2014; Ungar *et al.*, 2014).

Approximately 44 million people worldwide suffer from Alzheimer's disease or a related dementia, and only one in four people have been diagnosed (Alzheimer's

Disease International, n.d., cited in alzheimers.net, n.d.). In addition, Alzheimer's disease represents the top cause for disabilities in later life (Alzheimer's Disease International, n.d., cited in alzheimers.net, n.d.). In the case of ethnic groups, the incidence of Alzheimer's disease in relation to age is as follows: between 65 and 74 years old, 9.1 per cent are African American, whereas 2.9 per cent are white; between 75 and 84 years old, 27.9 per cent are Hispanic; and at 85 years old and above, 62.9 per cent are Hispanic, whereas 30.2 per cent are white. It is estimated that by 2050, 13.8 million people aged 65 and over will be diagnosed with Alzheimer's disease (Alzheimer's Disease International, n.d., cited in alzheimers.net, n.d.).

Regarding the mortality rate due to Alzheimer's disease, there was a 71 per cent increase in the USA between the years 2000 and 2013. Overall, Alzheimer's disease constitutes the only disease among the top 10 causes of death that cannot be prevented or cured and whose progression cannot be stopped (Alzheimer's Association, 2015).

Due to his profession and university medical training, James is aware of the epidemiology of Alzheimer's disease. He is more interested in learning about how patients experience the condition. This information will help him decide on his research questions.

The lived experience of Alzheimer's disease

Robinson *et al.* (2012) conducted a 3-year longitudinal study in Sweden aimed at exploring the lived experience of the early stage of Alzheimer's disease through the story of a 64-year-old woman. The participant was interviewed on four occasions at one-year intervals. The findings revealed that the early stage of Alzheimer's disease involved an outward route that required personal adjustment to the limitations posed by the disease itself. The overall experience was described as a reconciliation with the self and the illness, accompanied by a variety of coping mechanisms (e.g. acting as normal) and reactions (such as self-blame, perceiving the self as a burden to others, etc.) and evoking subsequent feelings; however, it was mainly perceived as continuous suffering.

A literature review conducted by Snyder (2001) in order to explore the feelings and subjective accounts of persons with Alzheimer's disease revealed several alterations to one's self due to the disease as well as a plethora of feelings connected with the symptoms and a variety of coping strategies. Admittedly, an alienation from the self and others was described by perceiving one's self as "vacant", "lost" and "a shell of one's former self" after the diagnosis. This detachment from oneself due to the disease's symptoms led to the loss of patients' sense of manhood in some cases, in that one perceived that he was no longer able to support his household (Snyder, 2001).

Further, a range of coping strategies seemed to be developed to cope with the disease, including denial, concealment of one's health condition to combat stigma, or revealing one's health condition to have support and safety. In relation to the patients' perception of symptoms, this led to several feelings arising, such as frustration over losing things, inability to trust oneself due to experiencing paranoia, anger due to the difficulty of accomplishing tasks and forgetting people, places or things, and mood fluctuations (Alzheimer's Association, 2015).

Similarly, a study conducted by Hedman *et al.* (2012) in Sweden aimed to explore the sense of self of 12 people living with Alzheimer's disease using Harré's theory and interviews, as well as an examination of their degree of cognitive impairment, using the Cognitive Performance Scale (CPS) (Morris *et al.*, 1994, cited in Hedman *et al.*, 2012). According to Harré (1998), there are three aspects of self: self No. 1, which encompasses expressions of the embodied experience of being a unique person and is presented using the first person expression; self No. 2, which encompasses a person's attributes and includes past, present and future attributes; and self No. 3, which incorporates the social component: an interaction between the way people express themselves to others (Selves No. 1 and No. 2), and the way others perceive them (Harré, 1998, p. 135, cited in Hedman *et al.*, 2012).

The findings of Hedman *et al.*'s study describe several alterations in self and life imposed by the disease. In relation to one's life, participants described a vivid life, in the sense that one perceived the self as more active (e.g. working, travelling), in contrast to life after the diagnosis, which is described as terminated or as a sentence. At the same time, feelings of despair and sadness emerged. This perception of life is accompanied with the devaluation of one's self as well as low self-esteem. However, for some participants, even if the condition was not irreversible, they believed that they could keep it under control (Hedman *et al.*, 2012). Furthermore, a range of coping strategies had also been reported, such as acting normal, similarly to the study of Robinson *et al.* (2012); taking notes; planning carefully; accepting help from others and being physically active (Hedman *et al.*, 2012).

Interestingly, there were some positive meanings attributed to Alzheimer's disease, as there were participants who described an adjustment in relation to their demands, as well as a feeling of gratitude towards their family because of the disease (Hedman *et al.*, 2012).

Discuss

- How could the brief review of the literature above help James?
- Could the existing literature help James refine his research question? How?

This brief overview of the lived experiences of Alzheimer's disease is very helpful for James, who would like to better understand how patients experience Alzheimer's disease. Since he wants to understand the experiences of many people, he decides to combine quantitative and qualitative research methodologies.

Through quantitative research, James will record patients' experiences on a larger scale, while qualitative research will allow him to understand patients' experiences in greater depth, thus enabling him to make better sense of the quantitative results. However, he has not finalised his research questions, and so he chooses to read up on mixed methodologies before he can refine his research ideas.

Qualitative vs. quantitative design

Quantitative design examines a phenomenon in terms of variables and relationships between measurements. It supports the idea that there is only one truth and one real world that someone can get to know and that the researcher gets to know the world through an empirical method (deductive approach) (Vrasidas, 2014). Therefore, it pre-structures data, research questions, conceptual frameworks and design. The sample is larger than in qualitative studies and generalisation is made based on sampling, while the phases of the study occur separately (Punch, 2005; Vrasidas, 2014).

Qualitative design, on the other hand, supports the idea that there are many truths and realities, and that the researcher gets to know the world through a variety of methods; for example, the scientific method, the biographical method, the artistic method and religion. The sample is usually small but the context of the study is immutable. The analysis of data is based on subjectivity and concerns the total exploration of the natural environment. The researcher exists as a tool within the research. Data collection involves multiple pages, the context of the study adjusts continuously and the stages of the study occur simultaneously (Vrasidas, 2014). Some key qualitative methods are semi-structured or unstructured interviews, focus group discussions, discourse analysis and semiotic analysis, and ethnographic methods, including participant observation (Spicer, 2012). Some key quantitative methods are structured interview survey, statistical analysis of secondary quantitative data, quantitative content analysis and structured observation (Spicer, 2012).

There are several advantages of using each of these methods. First, through quantitative data, researchers can make standardised, objective comparisons, as well as overall descriptions of situations or phenomena in a systematic and comparable way. Second, quantitative analysis is more objective, meaning that it does not depend on the researcher who is conducting the analysis (Punch, 2005). Similarly, there are some advantages to using qualitative methods. First, they are flexible in the sense that they can be used in a wider range of situations and for a wider range of purposes and they can be modified as the study progresses. They are well suited for studying naturally occurring, real-life situations. Second, they are of great importance and can be applied mainly when the researcher wants to explore the lived experience of a phenomenon, including people's meanings and purposes. Qualitative data also possess a holism and richness and can deal with the complexity of social phenomena (Punch, 2005).

When deciding which method to use, the following should be taken into consideration:

1 The researcher needs to link questions with method, which means using quantitative methods for quantitative questions and qualitative methods for qualitative questions.
2 Is the researcher interested in making standardised and systematic comparisons, therefore accounting for variance? Or is s/he interested in studying the phenomenon holistically and in its context, therefore finding out about the interpretations it has for the people involved and about their meanings and purposes, and trying to see what processes are involved?
3 The researcher needs to think about the available literature and its form. Is most of the information concerning the topic approached quantitatively or qualitatively in the literature?
4 The researcher needs to weigh and estimate the financial expenses and resources needed for each approach, as well as his/her own expertise with the methods.
5 The researcher needs to acknowledge which of the two methods will bring more insight to the research problem.
6 The researcher needs to simply choose the method that s/he prefers or enjoys (Punch, 2005).

What is a mixed method design?

In this section, we rely heavily on Creswell and Plano Clark's (2011) work, which is an excellent guide to mixed methodology. A mixed method design is a type of design that includes both quantitative methodology (statistical procedures) and qualitative methodology when designing and analysing a phenomenon under investigation (e.g. data collection, data analysis etc.). In particular, when using a mixed method design the data are collected and analysed using both qualitative and quantitative methods in relation to the research questions, and the data are mixed, combined or merged. In relation to the research aims, priority is given to either the quantitative or the qualitative form. Further, the procedures are used throughout the whole study or in parts of it and are designed and developed in relation to the theoretical background as well as the philosophical underpinnings. Overall, there is a combination of the procedures that direct how the study will be conducted (Creswell and Plano Clark, 2011).

When to use a mixed method design

There are a variety of research problems that could best be explored through a mixed method design (Creswell and Plano Clark, 2011). As an illustration, considering that qualitative findings are not easily generalised, a quantitative design is needed to strengthen the results of a study. Further, results could provide a partial explanation of the phenomenon under study and, in such a case, a mixed method approach is recommended. There might also be cases when researchers cannot define the research questions a priori, as well as the variables that should be measured, or the theoretical background that would sustain the study's rationale. In this case, it is recommended to start with a qualitative approach to address all these issues; this would be followed by a quantitative design to test whether the qualitative results could be generalised. Even in cases when a qualitative method is used, a quantitative method could then be used to enhance the understanding of some phase of the research. There have also been instances when the theoretical framework employed required data to be collected both quantitatively and qualitatively, simultaneously, and in order to build onto one another (Creswell and Plano Clark, 2011). Finally, there are cases where there is a need, especially with longitudinal studies, to connect several studies to achieve an objective; this could include studies that collect both quantitative and qualitative data at the same time or in sequence (Creswell and Plano Clark, 2011). Overall, to decide how the two methods will be connected, the researcher needs to consider the following three questions (Punch, 2005):

1 Will equal weight be given to the two approaches?
2 Will the two approaches be interactive or separate?
3 How will they be ordered?

Steps in conducting a mixed method study

As with all other designs, it is important that the research project's title reflects the research objectives by giving a clear statement about the research design. The title should be brief and concise, mention the topic being addressed, the study population and the setting of the study, and define the design by the word "mixed method", avoiding the terms "qualitative" and "quantitative" except when it is necessary to stress the priority given to one method over another.

Another key point is the preparation of a mixed method purpose statement, which should include the overall aim of the study; a detailed account of the type of mixed methods design involved, in order to introduce the reader to the specific type of methods that will be used, as well as provide a brief definition of the type of design; combined specific quantitative and qualitative purpose statements that clearly define the type of data to be collected, as well as the population under study and the settings for both the quantitative and the qualitative stages of the study; and a justification for collecting both quantitative and qualitative forms of data that is in line with the rationale for choosing this type of design (Creswell and Plano Clark, 2011).

The next step is to define the mixed methods research questions, which are proposed to be either predetermined and based on the literature or a specific clinical field (convergent design) or emergent, meaning that they could occur during the different phases of the research project. There are a variety of ways in which these questions could be written, including method-focused mixed methods research questions (both quantitative and qualitative data that are written in relation to the mixed methods design); content-focused mixed methods research questions (both quantitative and qualitative data in which the researcher makes explicit the content of the study and implies the research method); and combination mixed methods questions (the researcher clarifies both the methods and the content of the study) (Creswell and Plano Clark, 2011).

As far as data collection in mixed methods is concerned, several instruments may be used (e.g. diaries or photos in the case of the qualitative form and questionnaires that comply with the quantitative research questions). When it comes to sampling, it is proposed to use a combination of random (quantitative) and purposeful (qualitative) sampling (Creswell and Plano Clark, 2011).

James is more confident now and has a clear idea in mind about what he would like to study. He decides to start with a quantitative research methodology to measure the quality of life of patients living with Alzheimer's disease. This is because existing instruments cover all aspects of life, including the social, psychological, biological and so forth. Therefore, James will have the opportunity to study a representative sample of patients living with Alzheimer's disease and generalise the results to the relevant patient population. Based on the quantitative results, James will then conduct qualitative interviews to gain a deeper understanding of the quantitative findings. For the interviews, James will follow designated procedures and check for data saturation to make sure that he has gathered enough data. Therefore, James refines his research questions to the following: What is the quality of life of patients living with Alzheimer's disease, and how can the patients' quality of life be explained from the patients' perspective?

Types of mixed methods designs

Dominant mixed method designs include triangulation design, embedded design, explanatory design and exploratory design (Creswell and Plano Clark, 2011). The most widely known design is triangulation, which is selected when the researcher uses both qualitative and quantitative methods in order to confirm, cross-validate or corroborate findings within a single study (Creswell, 2013). The triangulation method includes the simultaneous collection of both qualitative and quantitative data in one phase of the study. Therefore, quantitative data could be collected first, before all the qualitative data are collected. The interpretation of the findings places emphasis on existing knowledge or provides an explanation of any gap in the data collection that might emerge.

Triangulation is mainly used to cross-check results for consistency and to control any bias that concerns either the qualitative or the quantitative approach (Spicer, 2012). According to Denzin (1978), there are four types of triangulation:

- data triangulation, which includes diverse sources of data, in order for the researcher to examine the phenomenon in different settings and in different points in time so that in-depth descriptions of the phenomenon can occur
- investigator triangulation, which means a research team is used, with multiple observers in the field, engaging in discussions concerning the differences

found in the data from their point of view, as well as similarities, which can reduce personal biases
- theory triangulation, where researchers approach data with several hypotheses in mind in order to see how each best fits the data
- methodological triangulation, which might usually combine ethnographic observations with interviews and can be used as a rationale for mixing qualitative and quantitative methods in a study

It must be noted that there is variation in the triangulation design: the convergence model, the data transformation model, the validating quantitative data model and the multilevel model (Creswell and Plano Clark, 2011). Researchers using a convergence model for data collection simultaneously collect quantitative and qualitative data, although data analysis is performed at different stages and the two datasets are then combined. However, the researcher should take into consideration the specific sample to be used, meaning that they should decide whether the sample will be the same or will differ in the quantitative and qualitative forms. If the researcher wants to compare the datasets, s/he should use the same individuals. Furthermore, the researcher should decide on the sample size for both forms of data and the decision should be justified (e.g. if the size is not equal, this should be recognised as a limitation). If the aim is to assess the same concept in both forms, then parallel research questions should be used for data collection (Creswell and Plano Clark, 2011). In addition, the researcher should decide whether the data will be collected from two independent sources or from a single source; it is recommended that they are collected independently from two sources.

On the other hand, the transformation model involves the separate collection and analysis of qualitative and quantitative data. Nevertheless, analysis is performed to transform one data type into the other data type, and this is achieved by either quantifying qualitative findings or qualifying quantitative results in order to compare, interrelate and further analyse the two data sets. The validating quantitative data model is used to validate and expand the quantitative findings from a survey through the inclusion of a few open-ended qualitative questions by collecting both qualitative and quantitative data within one survey instrument, thus providing the researcher with quotes that can be used to validate and enrich the quantitative survey findings (Creswell and Plano Clark, 2011).

The multilevel model encompasses different methods (quantitative and qualitative) in order to address different levels within a system. Then, the findings from each level are combined into an overall interpretation. As far as the explanatory design is concerned, sampling is done over two phases: the quantitative phase and the qualitative phase. However, they are related to each other and build on one another (Creswell and Plano Clark, 2011). When using an explanatory design, it is recommended that the researcher selects the same participants for both forms, and then if s/he wants to follow up with some qualitative research, the participants selected should be chosen based on the initial quantitative results (Creswell and Plano Clark, 2011).

In exploratory design, the collection and analysis of qualitative data precedes the quantitative phase, which is used to build on the qualitative phase. However, sampling occurs in two phases that are related to each other. There are also cases, when implementing an exploratory design, where a three-phase model is used, whereby an instrument design phase follows the initial, exploratory phase, and this is then followed by a phase involving the testing and administering of the instrument (Creswell and Plano Clark, 2011).

As far as the number of participants is concerned, in exploratory design, it is recommended to use a different sample in the quantitative phase than in the qualitative phase and to obtain a large sample. Further, regarding the qualitative results used to inform the quantitative data collection, it is recommended to use themes, codes and quotes in order to design the instrument and to use rigorous procedures, as well as to provide a thorough explanation of the whole procedure followed (Creswell and Plano Clark, 2011).

Embedded design uses both qualitative and quantitative data that are collected in a predetermined ordered sequence, or in parallel, or in both forms (Creswell and Plano Clark, 2011). With embedded design, the researcher needs to provide the rationale for nesting the data as well as to take into consideration the time needed for nesting the data. In addition, to avoid bias, secondary data should be collected through diaries or during an experiment. Moreover, to anticipate any further issues arising during data collection, the researcher should further examine the literature (Creswell and Plano Clark, 2011).

Additionally, there are other approaches proposed for combining qualitative and quantitative methods, which include the following (Punch, 2005):

- Qualitative research facilitates quantitative research: qualitative research could be used for background information on the context, and subjects could act as a source of hypotheses and aid scale construction.
- Quantitative research facilitates qualitative research: quantitative research helps with the selection of participants for a qualitative investigation.
- The combination of both quantitative and qualitative research aims to provide a general picture: quantitative research is used to fill in the gaps left from qualitative research, or when it is not possible to address all issues with one of the two approaches, a combination is needed.
- Structure and process: quantitative research is efficient at getting to the "structural features" of social life, while qualitative studies are usually stronger in terms of "processual" aspects.
- Researchers' and subjects' perspectives: to put together researchers' concerns (quantitative research) and subjects' personal experiences as a starting point (qualitative research). Qualitative research may facilitate the interpretations of relationships between variables: qualitative study can help to explain the reasons for the relationships between variables found from a quantitative study.
- Relationship between macro and micro levels: macro levels are examined through quantitative research and large-scale, structural features of social

life, while qualitative research tends to address small-scale, behavioural aspects.
- Stage in the research process: quantitative and qualitative research may be appropriate for different stages within a longitudinal study.
- Hybrids: qualitative research is conducted within a quasi-experimental research design.

Discuss

- How could James select the most appropriate mixed method design?
- Which mixed method design better suits James' study?

James will use the explanatory design, as he will start with a quantitative study and then conduct in-depth interviews to better understand his quantitative findings. This is a good way to support in-depth understanding of numerical data without leaving the researcher speculating or wondering about what other research could be done in order to answer the inexplicable.

Advantages and disadvantages of the dominant mixed method designs

Triangulation design

Data can be collected at one time and not simultaneously, and employees from several backgrounds can be employed. However, there might be a case in which qualitative and quantitative data are distinct from one other, and this would require the collection of additional data. The decision here lies in what type of data should be collected (qualitative or quantitative) or the re-examination of existing data, which would be more time consuming (Creswell and Plano Clark, 2011). Additionally, there is the "philosophical critique" of triangulation design, which underlines that even if different methods generate consistent findings, it is by no means certain that a further method would not reveal different, contradictory findings (Seale, 1999, cited in Spicer, 2012).

Embedded design

Embedded design can save a lot of time, as collecting data can take a series of forms. Furthermore, it could be a source of fundraising, since it is quantitative in nature (experiment or correlational analysis). Nevertheless, there are also some challenges when using this kind of design. The researcher must be very specific when defining the purpose of collecting either qualitative or quantitative data that would be part of a larger quantitative or qualitative study, and this must be indicated in the primary and secondary aims of the study. Also, it might be difficult to integrate the two methods, which are used to answer different research questions; however, there is the option of using both datasets when writing the results or publishing them in different papers. Above all, the researchers must estimate the time required to collect and analyse quantitative data in relation to the larger qualitative design in the case of experimental designs with embedded qualitative data (Creswell, 2005).

Explanatory design

The advantages of explanatory design lie in the fact that it is a two-phase structure that is easy to implement, since data collection takes place in distinct phases and only one type of data is collected at a time; thus, there is no need for additional human resources when implementing the design. Regarding the final report, the qualitative part could be written first and then the quantitative or vice versa, so it saves time for the researcher. In addition, it could be used in multiphase investigations and single mixed method studies. In general, this design is more quantitatively oriented. Still, it is considered to be time consuming as far as its implementation is concerned, and the researcher should a priori decide whether s/he should use the same individuals for both phases, use participants from the same sample for both phases, or draw participants from the same population for the two phases (Creswell and Plano Clark, 2011). Additionally, it would be difficult for a student to select this kind of mixed method design, since the study should be approved for implementation by a review board and, in this case, the student would not be in a position to respond about the sample size for the second phase (Creswell and Plano Clark, 2011).

Exploratory design

Explanatory design is considered to be easy to implement and analyse and, therefore, could be implemented in multiphase research studies as well as in single studies (Creswell and Plano Clark, 2011). Despite its advantages, there are also some disadvantages: it can be time consuming and the procedures relating to the quantitative phase cannot be fully explained for approval; thus, a tentative plan should be designed (Creswell and Plano Clark, 2011).

Deciding on which type of mixed method design to use

Creswell (2013) outlined four steps to deciding on the type of mixed method design to use. First, researchers should use a single design in line with their research problem in order to be in a position to manage the whole procedure. Second, researchers should weigh their skills when deciding whether to use qualitative or quantitative methods. If they feel that they do not have sufficient knowledge and expertise in one method, they could work in a team or select a design that does not emphasise that method. Third, they should carefully explore the availability of the resources needed (time, funding, etc.). Fourth, selection could also be based on the end-user's demands.

Additionally, the decision should be based on timing (the time required for data collection, data analysis and reporting of the data) and weighting: this means that the researcher weights the priorities that should be given to either method for answering the research questions. Therefore, it could be that both methods were equal or unequal in addressing the research problem. Furthermore, weighting is affected by the goals, the research questions and the use of procedures from research traditions (e.g. quantitative experimental designs or qualitative case study designs). As might be expected, the available resources could influence weighting. For example, if resources are available, both types could be implemented at the same time. Now, in the case that the researcher is more familiar with qualitative research than with quantitative research, s/he would choose appropriately. Another possibility would be that priority might be given to one method over the other in relation to the preferences of journal editors, reviewers and funding officers. Overall, weighting strategies should be defined and justified in the written reports in a clear manner: in the title, in relation to the chosen theoretical background and within the methods section (Creswell and Plano Clark, 2011).

The decision on which type of mixed method design to choose could also depend on the way both methods would be mixed. There are several strategies that could be used for mixing qualitative and quantitative data, including merging them (that is, the datasets are brought together or integrated). The merging of the data could take place during the interpretation of the findings (the analysis is conducted separately and they are merged in the interpretation or discussion section) or even during analysis (by transforming one into another or consolidating the data into new variables).

Conclusion

This chapter focused on the use of mixed methodology for studying and understanding the quality of life of patients living with Alzheimer's disease. James chose a combination of quantitative and qualitative methodologies because he wanted generalisable results, on the one hand, and on the other hand, a deeper understanding of his patients' experiences. Thus, a mixed methodology design can give James the opportunity to achieve a more holistic understanding of his patients' experiences while addressing his research questions more adequately.

References

Altmann A, Tian LL, Henderson VW and Greicius MD (2014) Alzheimer's disease neuroimaging initiative. Sex modifies the APOErelated risk of developing Alzheimer disease. *Annals of Neurology* 75(4): 563–573.

Alzheimer's Association (2015) Alzheimer's disease facts and figures. *Alzheimer's & Dementia* 11(3): 332.

Alzheimer's.net (n.d.) 2015 Alzheimer's Statistics. Available online from: www.alzheimers.net/resources/alzheimers-statistics/. Accessed 3 February 2016.

American Psychiatric Association (2013) *Diagnostic and Statistical Manual of Mental Disorders* (5th ed.). Washington, DC: American Psychiatric Publishing.

Creswell JW (2013) *Research Design. Qualitative, Quantitative and Mixed Methods Approaches* (4th ed.). Los Angeles: SAGE.

Creswell JW and Plano Clark VL (2011) *Designing and Conducting Mixed Methods Research* (2nd ed.). Los Angeles: SAGE.

Denzin NK (1978) *The Research Act: A Theoretical Introduction to Sociological Methods* (3rd ed.). New York: McGraw-Hill.

Di Marco LY, Marzo A, Muñoz-Ruiz M, Ikram MA, Kivipelto M and Ruefenacht D (2014) Modifiable lifestyle factors in dementia: A systematic review of longitudinal observational cohort studies. *Journal of Alzheimers Disease* 42(1): 119–135.

Hebert LE, Weuve J, Scherr PA and Evans DA (2013) Alzheimer disease in the United States (2010–2050) estimated using the 2010 Census. *Neurology* 80(19): 1778–1783.

Hedman R, Hansebo G, Ternestedt BM, Hellström I and Norberg A (2012) How people with Alzheimer's disease express their sense of self: Analysis using Rom Harré's theory of selfhood. *Dementia* 12(6): 713–733.

Loef M and Walach H (2013) Midlife obesity and dementia: Meta-analysis and adjusted forecast of dementia prevalence in the United States and China. *Obesity* 21(1): E51–5.

Loy CT, Schofield PR, Turner AM and Kwok JBJ (2014) Genetics of dementia. *Lancet* 383: 828–840.

Meng XF, Yu JT, Wang HF, Tan MS, Wang C, Tan CC and Tan L (2014) Midlife vascular risk factors and the risk of Alzheimer's disease: A systematic review and meta-analysis. *Journal of Alzheimer's Disease* 42(4): 1295–1310.

Morse J (1991) On the evaluation of qualitative proposals. *Qualitative Health Research* 1(2): 147–151.

Ninomiya T, Ohara T, Hirakawa Y, Yoshida D, Doi Y and Hata J (2011) Midlife and late-life blood pressure and dementia in Japanese elderly: The Hisayama Study. *Hypertension* 58(1): 22–28.

Punch KF (2013) *Introduction to Social Research: Quantitative and Qualitative Approaches*. London: SAGE.

Robinson P, Giorgi B and Sirkka-Liisa E (2012) The lived experience of early-stage Alzheimer's disease: A three year longitudinal phenomenological case study. *Journal of Phenomenological Psychology* 43(2): 216–238.

Rönnemaa E, Zethelius B, Lannfelt L and Kilander L (2011) Vascular risk factors and dementia: 40-year follow-up of a population-based cohort. *Dementia and Geriatric Cognitive Disorders* 31(6): 460–466.

Rusanen M, Kivipelto M, Quesenberry CP, Zhou J and Whitmer RA (2011) Heavy smoking in midlife and long-term risk of Alzheimer disease and vascular dementia. *Archives of Internal Medicine* 171(4): 333–339.

Snyder L (2001) The lived experience of Alzheimer's. Understanding the feelings and subjective accounts of persons with the disease. *Alzheimer's Care Quarterly* 22(2): 8–22.

Spicer N (2012) Combining qualitative and quantitative methods. In: Spicer, C. (ed.) *Researching Society and Culture*. London: SAGE, pp. 480–493.

Stern Y (2012) Cognitive reserve in ageing and Alzheimer's disease. *The Lancet Neurology* 11(11): 1006–1012.

Ungar L, Altmann A and Greicius MD (2014) Apolipoprotein E, gender, and Alzheimer's disease: An overlooked, but potent and promising interaction. *Brain Imaging and Behavior* 8(2): 262–273.

Vrasidas C (2014) *Introduction to Qualitative Research*. [E-reader version] Cardet Press. ISBN: 978-9963-2802-3-0.

10 Ethics in research
Breast cancer

Abstract

A postgraduate student, Mary Hanson, is about to begin her research on women living with breast cancer, focusing on the impact the disease has had on their relationship with their partners. Mary has obtained approval from institutional and national ethics committees, but she is slightly embarrassed when one of her participants, Andrea Richards, asks the following questions after reading the informed consent form: "Will you record the interviews or will you take notes? How long will you keep your data? Will somebody else read my interview? I am sorry but I cannot sign the form without knowing this information."

In this last chapter, the principles of ethics in research are explained and applied to the case of researching breast cancer in order to highlight that ethics in research are important and necessary for the protection of both the researcher and the research participants. The chapter focuses on the sensitive areas of human rights and dignity and emphasises that research is possible only if it respects and benefits research participants and humanity.

Learning objectives:

- Explain why breast cancer is a sensitive issue to study.
- Describe the main principles of ethics in research.
- Explain the importance of informed consent.

Scenario

Mary Hanson is a postgraduate student and wants to begin her research on women living with breast cancer, focusing on the impact the disease had on their relationship with their partners. Mary has obtained approval from institutional and national ethics committees, but she is slightly embarrassed when one of her participants, Andrea Richards, asks the following questions after reading the informed consent form: "Could you please clarify why you are doing this study as it is not very clear to me?", "Will you record the interviews or will you take notes? How long will you keep your data? Will somebody else read my interview? I am sorry but I cannot sign the form without knowing this information. I suffered cancer, I had my breast removed, I lost my hair, I was under severe stress. I do not want to go through something stressful."

Mary is puzzled. She cannot understand why her participant will not sign the informed consent form, since she obtained all the necessary approvals from the various ethics committees. As she is at the initial stages of her research, Mary delves more deeply into the literature in order to understand whether she missed something important when preparing the informed consent form. Her participant raised sensitive issues about the safekeeping of data and ensuring anonymity, as well as issues pertaining to the impact of cancer on patients' emotional wellbeing and social life. Thus, Mary tried to revisit articles that focused on the psychosocial consequences of breast cancer to make sense of her participants' behaviour and decide on her next step forward.

Discuss

- What might be the psychosocial impacts of breast cancer?
- How could the psychosocial consequences of breast cancer influence a patient's understanding of her participation in research?

The psychosocial consequences of breast cancer

There is evidence to suggest that breast cancer is a complicated experience because patients may go through different emotional and social stages. More specifically, patients go through physiological changes and demanding treatment and may experience life restrictions. Furthermore, they are likely to experience anxiety and depression, which can cause deterioration in the course of treatment (Jassin and Whitford, 2014). Jassin and Whitford (2014) conducted 12 qualitative interviews with Bahraini women and tried to gauge the complexity in the illness experience of breast cancer. They found that some patients experienced fear of death and chemotherapy, while others did not regard cancer as different from other conditions. Jassin and Whitford's patients experienced physical, emotional and psychological changes and they were particularly disappointed with their bodies, especially after having their breasts removed. Patients turned to family for support, though some patients were concerned about their husband's views and behaviour and worried that their husbands might look for another wife. On this note, they also sought comfort in religion and spirituality, especially when searching for a reason why they might have developed cancer. Believing that the disease was God's will helped some patients make sense of their cancer. Interestingly, the head scarf was turned into a tool for protection, as it served two functions. First, it had a religious value and it protected their feminine virtue. Second, it hid the side effects of chemotherapy, specifically hair loss.

Cancer has more specific effects on patients, such as fatigue, decreased sexual desire, psychological adjustment and problems in family relations. Bower *et al.* (2000) studied the experience of fatigue among almost 2,000 breast cancer patients using standardised questionnaires. Patients with breast cancer were found to be more fatigued, while one-third of patients reported being severely fatigued. The study also found that fatigue was associated with depression, pain and sleep disturbance. Also, patients who experienced fatigue were going through menopause and were undergoing chemotherapy.

Sexuality may also be influenced by cancer disease and treatment. Takahashi and Kai (2005) interviewed 21 Japanese patients with breast cancer to understand patients' experiences of sexuality. The authors presented the following interesting findings. First, patients were hesitant to continue having sex as they had prior to their diagnosis. Second, they experienced sexual changes after treatment, such as decreased desire for sexual activity. Third, coping with any changes experienced was a stressful task. Fourth, patients' relationships with their partners were under threat/strain. Apart from any physical changes due to the disease and the side effects of treatment, patients experienced depression, which had a negative impact on their desire for sexual activity.

In the literature, the psychological impact is very important in the lives of patients. To understand how patients adjust psychologically, Ching *et al.* (2012) interviewed 35 Chinese patients with breast cancer. The authors found that patients experienced disruption of their routine and they initially dealt with such a disruption by denying the existence of the condition. Later, patients adopted specific strategies for adjusting psychologically; that is, some of them focused on achievable goals. The authors identified different types of adjusters. Fighters accepted cancer and aimed to take control of their condition and treatment. Followers focused on coping and did not try to have full control. They could not accept cancer, and they were particularly stressed by the current problems deriving from the disease or by any future problems. Bearers placed emphasis on problems and did not accept the condition. They generally felt powerless and that their problems could not be managed. Despite the differences observed, all patients tried to maintain hope, find new meaning in life, minimise the impact of cancer and find the courage to carry on. Furthermore, they changed their way of thinking, became more sensitive to others' needs and appreciated life more.

Family relations may be jeopardised when a member is diagnosed with breast cancer. There is evidence to suggest that social support helps patients react to stress more effectively and keeps them from experiencing depression (Pistrand *et al.*, 1997). Mackenzie (2014) argued that cancer complicates social relationships within a family, and that patients younger than 50 years old have more social problems and may be sick over a longer period, because the psychosocial impact of cancer is greater on them since they have more social obligations to fulfil. To further investigate the complexities of relationships within the family, Mackenzie conducted 32 qualitative interviews in order to understand how patients with breast cancer managed the demands of work, family and healthcare. The findings showed that patients tended to prioritise self-healthcare over work and to prioritise family over care. Trying to bridge the three dimensions was not an easy task and some patients found it a struggle.

It seems that prioritising family over care is an issue for many patients. More specifically, Davey *et al.* (2012) conducted focus groups with patients with breast cancer to explore how patients cared for their children aged between 11 and 18. The authors found that patients needed to protect their children and they tried to control their reactions as much as they could. The idea here was that if they looked fine, then their children would be alright too. They also wanted to minimise the impact of cancer on their daily routine and avoided burdening their children in any way. Since parents were concerned with how their children understood and dealt with cancer, they chose to be open with their children and to explain to them all they needed to know. Some other parents used the experience of cancer as a teaching resource to explain to their children how to appreciate life more and how to cope with stressful events in life. Finally, many parents received support from their children. It seems here that children were involved in understanding, treating and coping with breast cancer. Interestingly, Wolf (2014) explained how families "cope communally with breast cancer", which means that they aligned their perception and action in such a way as to cope with the disease in a similar way. Through conducting 64 interviews, Wolf found that families changed their way of thinking, thought that cancer turned people into patients, and did not want to continue the role of being sick. Some families regarded cancer as something that had come to an end, while others viewed it as something that was life-long.

As patients with breast cancer go through these experiences, they construct their own story, which they narrate to either researchers or other people. Thomas-MacLean (2004) used data from 12 in-depth interviews and found that patients with breast cancer use Frank's narrative types: "reinstitution", "chaos" and "quest". Through the narrative of reinstitution, patients explained that they wanted to return to their pre-cancer life. In the chaos narrative, patients focused on their difficulties and suffering. Patients used the quest narrative to inform others that they had experienced a change in their life, in themselves and in their way of thinking. MacLean found that while all his patients used a variety of narratives, chaos dominated in the patients' stories. Utilising the chaos narrative and expressing feelings of suffering echoes other studies, which focused on how patients use survivorship in their stories. Kaiser (2008) interviewed 39 patients who had been diagnosed with breast cancer in the last 3 to 18 months prior to the interview. The survivor identity was not adopted by all patients. Some considered themselves as survivors in the sense that they had fought cancer and won. Others used survivorship as a pathway through which they had become stronger. Interestingly, some patients did not understand themselves as survivors, because they thought that the cancer might return. They described themselves as "cancer free for now" (p. 84). MacLean also found that age played a role in how patients understood surviving cancer. Survivorship among older patients was not an issue at all because they understood it as a disease that they would possibly develop in the third age. Bruke *et al.* (2012) relied on observation and in-depth interviews to understand how

Filipinas in the USA experienced cancer and made use of survivorship. The study revealed the following:

- Filipinas considered cancer as one of many trials experienced in their host country. For example, raising their children in the USA was indeed a trial and a struggle for them. On this note, they argued that surviving was for their children and not for themselves.
- Family dynamics within the family changed due to cancer in the sense that responsibilities were reallocated to family members.
- Some other patients took the experience of cancer as an opportunity to change their previous way of life.

Having assessed the illness experience of breast cancer, it is interesting to understand what happens when cancer returns. Sarenmalm *et al.* (2009: 1119) interviewed 40 patients who experienced breast cancer recurrence. Cancer recurrence seems to be a very stressful experience. The authors found three main experiences. First, patients "confronted cancer" and changed their view that they were cured. They rearranged their view of cancer from a potential threat to a real threat. Second, patients "struggled with their illness and eased distress" because they felt they were no longer happy and feelings of fear arose. Third, patients "transcended" by finding new meaning in life and by changing their understanding of themselves.

How patients experience breast cancer does not only depend on the nature of the disease or the people surrounding patients. It may be influenced structurally. Klawiter (2004) described in detail the experiences of one patient and argued that social movements and patient groups may influence the way patients experience their disease. More specifically, patient groups help patients improve, deal with the stigma and, thus, open up and change the way they think about the disease. The structural construction of the illness experience of breast cancer has been enhanced by the various information campaigns about the disease, its treatment and the available screening programmes. It is so strong and developed that it may cause patients with other types of cancer to feel stigmatised or to use breast cancer as a basis for describing their own experiences. For example, Bell (2014) explained that the experience of cancer has been "breast-cancer-ised", meaning that patients use breast cancer as a framework for narrating their own experiences with cancer.

Bell conducted 32 in-depth interviews with patients with cancer and aimed to understand how patients used survivorship. Bell found that survivorship was linked with breast cancer more often than with any other type of cancer. Furthermore, patients used breast cancer as a threshold for understanding their condition as good or bad. This was particularly the case with a few types of cancer, such as lung and cervical cancer, which have become stigmatised due to their association with smoking and sexual promiscuity, respectively. Interestingly, breast cancer has been understood as a threshold of suffering. Bell used the term "hierarchies of suffering" to point out that some patients thought that people with breast cancer did not suffer as much as people with other types of cancer because they could be cured. Other patients thought the opposite due to the possibility of patients with breast cancer needing to have their breasts removed; though they survived, they would encounter more emotional, psychological and family issues than survivors of other types of cancers.

> **Discuss**
>
> - What could Mary learn from the literature?
> - Are there any ethical issues that are applicable to research?
> - Mary's participant, Andrea, raised some critical questions. Which ethical principles do these questions relate to?

Ethics in research

The literature described shows that living with breast cancer is a stressful experience due to the multilayered consequences for both patients and their families. Thus, participating in research as a patient with breast cancer is not the same as a healthy individual participating in market research. Researchers may need to pay more attention to patients and be more careful and considerate about issues such as the vulnerability of patients, the pressure that patients may feel to participate in research, and any circumstances that patients may find disturbing or uncomfortable. This means that studying patients with chronic illness may raise more ethical issues that researchers may need to address (Campbell-Crofts *et al.*, 2013). Let us now look more deeply into the reasons why research should be ethical and what ethical principles studies should meet.

In 1963, Milgram published his research on the pressure that authority can exert on people to do things that they would not do otherwise. The research aimed at understanding the reasons behind Nazi atrocities and showing that the Nazis were not innately inhuman but were behaving based on authoritative orders. To prove his hypothesis, Milgram designed a laboratory experiment in which research participants played teachers who were punishing students who gave wrong answers to questions by giving them electric shocks. Though the electric shocks were fake, research participants were not aware of this critical piece of information, while the punished learners had been instructed to express their pain when electricity supposedly travelled through their body. The intensity of the electric shocks was gradually increased with each incorrect answer. Milgram was instructing the research participants, informing them when to administer the shocks. Milgram discovered that his research participants obeyed his orders, and this shed further light on the behaviour of Nazis under circumstances of pressure exerted by authority figures. Milgram's study is quite well known in psychology and is widely taught; however, Milgram might not have been able to conduct such a study nowadays, as it would violate fundamental ethical principles, such as informed consent.

Diener and Crandall (1978) explained that there are four main ethical principles in social research: harm to participants, informed consent, privacy and deception. These principles are widely found in research nowadays and it would be helpful to review each one separately. In this section, we rely heavily on the *European Textbook on Ethics in Research* (2010), which constitutes an excellent overview of the ethical principles in research.

Discuss

- Could Mary have violated any of the principles above, thereby causing Andrea to refuse to sign the informed consent form?
- If yes, how could Mary fix this?

Harm to participants

Research should not harm participants in either a direct or an indirect way. This may refer to physical harm, psychological distress, loss of self-esteem and so forth. Direct means of harm would be putting participants in circumstances where they could be physically hurt, such as requiring them to engage in a fight to study elements of verbal and non-verbal masculinity. Furthermore, participants could be directly harmed psychologically by making them feel useless or by underestimating their claimed achievements. There are indirect ways through which participants can be harmed psychologically. For example, a question about losing a beloved close relative may severely upset a participant. The issue of indirect psychological harm relates closely to the terms of vulnerability. The *European Textbook on Ethics in Research* (2010) defines vulnerable subjects "as those whose particular susceptibility to harm and exploitation and inability to protect their own interests results from factors over and above those resulting from the research setting itself". The *Textbook* carries on by clarifying that there are three main indicators of vulnerability. First, participants who are not competent cannot protect themselves and their interests and, therefore, are vulnerable. Second, when participants do not have clear information about the study they are participating in, they may not be able to protect themselves by withdrawing from the study. Third, age, disability and illness are experiences that may make participants vulnerable due to psychosocial and physical implications, such as restricted lives, depression and so forth. However, vulnerability is not a fixed experience and may differ according to participants' health conditions. For example, terminally ill people are more vulnerable because they are less likely to withstand pressure from others (*European Textbook on Ethics in Research*, 2010). A way of minimising potential harm and vulnerability is to adequately inform potential participants about the nature of the study and ask them to sign an informed consent form.

Andrea, Mary's participant, may be considered as a vulnerable individual. This is because Andrea was suffering a life-threatening condition and difficult treatment, including surgery and chemotherapy, which made her less able to control her own interests. Revisiting the review of the literature as presented earlier in the chapter, patients with breast cancer experience physical, emotional and psychological problems, fatigue, sexual problems and issues with family relations.

Patients with breast cancer may experience severe stress, which can lead to depression and sleep disturbance. Moreover, patients' daily routine is disrupted due to fatigue, stress and treatment, while patients may rearrange their view of themselves as useless or dying persons. The literature also shows that family relations change in the sense that patients may feel that they are an extra burden. Hair loss and breast removal are traumatic experiences for the individual, as women may feel less attractive or that they have lost their feminine role within the family.

Interestingly, Andrea is vulnerable not only because she has gone through a life-threatening disease but also because of the possibility of recurrence, which is a very stressful experience. In the event of recurrence, patients may feel that their life is coming to an end, and all the anxiety and stress are exacerbated. Having gone through such an intensely stressful experience, Andrea is a vulnerable research subject for various reasons. First, she may experience stress or upheaval during the interviews should any of the questions be too sensitive. Mary could deal with such a situation by informing Andrea about the possibility of having to answer some sensitive questions and signpost during the interview in order to prepare Andrea for what will follow in the interview. Also, Mary could remind Andrea at the beginning of the interview that she is free to choose not to answer any of the questions posed. Second, Andrea may feel unnecessary pressure to participate in the study to help research come up with a beneficial outcome for patients. On this note, Mary should avoid any emotionally loaded words in the informed consent form and clarify that participation is only voluntary. Third, Andrea may be afraid that refusal to participate would affect her treatment. Mary should assure Andrea in writing that this will not happen in the case that Andrea opts out of the study. It is worth noting that the informed consent form is a very useful document that works like a contract between researchers and research participants.

Informed consent

Informed consent relies on specific ethical principles (*European Textbook on Ethics in Research*, 2010). These are respect for autonomy, respect for dignity and respect for persons. Apart from respect, an informed consent form should provide detailed information, individuals should be aware that signing it is purely voluntary, and they should be competent enough to understand its content in order to sign it. Regarding detailed information, an informed consent form should clearly explain to the participants the purpose of the research; the participants' role; that participants do not have to sign and consent; that regardless of their signature, they can withdraw their participation at any time they wish; that they may file any complaints about the research procedure; that confidentiality will be maintained; and that they may ask to have a summary of the research results. The consent form should be written in plain language without any jargon or unclear sentences. The information should be very clear to potential participants so that they can fully understand the purpose of the study and their role and, therefore, sign voluntarily.

Voluntariness is a critical aspect of giving consent. Potential participants should not be under any kind of pressure to sign the consent form. Pressure could be direct, such as "you have to participate; this is an important study", or indirect, along the lines of "the study will benefit patients a great deal". Such statements, which could be verbal or written in the consent form, could exert pressure on potential participants and may make them feel stigmatised if they do not sign, because they do not want to give the impression that they do not wish to help research that could benefit specific groups in society (i.e. the development of new medication for x disease).

Another important aspect of informed consent is competence. Potential participants should be competent enough to understand all the information that is included in the consent form in order to sign voluntarily. Potential participants should be adults and mentally competent to be able to sign. In the case of children or mentally ill people, guardians must be adequately informed and should sign on behalf of the child or the mentally ill individual. There are cases in which the child or mentally ill person is asked to provide consent orally in addition to the signed consent of the guardian. Andrea is an adult and able to read, understand and sign an informed consent form. However, she feels that there are gaps in the informed consent form, as important information is missing. More specifically, Andrea wants to know the exact purpose of the study and also has questions about issues of confidentiality and privacy. Since the informed consent form was lacking this information, Andrea might have felt unsafe and somewhat deceived. Informed consent works like a contract between her and Mary but Andrea does not feel comfortable enough to sign a contract that would bind her to commitments that she is not aware of from the beginning.

Privacy and confidentiality

Andrea highlighted the issues of confidentiality and privacy. She wanted to know who else might have access to the data and how long Mary planned on keeping the data for. However, why does Andrea want to know about privacy and confidentiality? This is because privacy and confidentiality are supplementary elements of the main principle of protecting the person. Privacy, according to the *European Textbook on Ethics in Research* (2010: 78–79), refers to the protection of "control over information about oneself, control over access to oneself, both physical and mental, and control over one's ability to make important decisions about family and lifestyle in order to be self-expressive and to develop varied relationships". In other words, privacy has to do with intrusion into an individual's personal information and space. Confidentiality focuses more on the issue of protecting information that is specific to the individual and might be harmful for the individual should it be released to other people or the public.

Ensuring complete privacy may not be feasible in all types of research. For example, in long-standing ethnographic studies, ethnographers will have to make visits to various potential informants and start observing and asking questions without prior warning or information about the study. In practice, it would be difficult to inform all potential informants in a community before ethnographers could start their study. Also, observing a community is a very dynamic task, and ethnographers may decide to change course based on the findings they have so far.

Andrea wants to know about the people who will have access to the data and that confidentiality can be maintained. Confidentiality is very important in a research context because it helps participants feel safe. Andrea had her breast removed, lost her hair and went through changing her self-image as well as social reactions such as stigmatisation. Thus, she does not want to put herself in an upsetting situation. Given her experiences, Andrea is a vulnerable subject, and ensuring confidentiality is even more imperative in her case so that she may be persuaded to participate in the study.

Deception

Since Andrea had gone through such psychosocial disruption, the missing information from the informed consent form made her suspicious of the actual purpose of the study. Before signing the informed consent form, Andrea wanted to make sure that there was no intent of deception. Deception refers to presenting one's research as something that it is not. Deception has not only been observed in Milgram's experiment but has been widely used in social sciences, such as in psychology experiments. The argument in favour of deception is that participants answer more naturally when they do not know detailed information about the study. However, the argument against it is that deception is wrong by nature and that it violates fundamental ethical principles, such as that of informed consent and voluntariness and potential harm (Bryman, 2001). Thus, a study that relies on deceiving patients will face serious difficulties in obtaining approval from ethics committees.

Avoiding complete deception may be a challenge in qualitative research, which relies on in-depth interviews and observation. Though the purpose of a qualitative study rarely changes during research, researchers may come up with questions that may be more sensitive to potential participants, making it seem as though the study has changed direction or focus. The way out of such a potential misunderstanding between participants and researchers is to inform potential participants in the informed consent form that more questions may come up during the study that might be sensitive to participants. The consent form should clarify that participants can refuse to answer any question. Therefore, the informed consent form is critical for minimising the suspicions of deception and, once again, works like a contract between researchers and participants.

Other ethical issues

All research needs to be reviewed independently by ethics committees in order to obtain final approval to start the research study. Research committees are very important institutions and work as protective mechanisms for both research participants and researchers. Committees may ask researchers to take additional ethical actions, which fall under the principles of protecting and respecting the persons. For example, researchers may need to clarify how they are going to keep their data safe, where the raw data will be kept, how electronic data will be kept safely, who will have access to the data, how long it will be kept for, how researchers will destroy the data and so forth. To regulate the operation of ethics committees, many countries have passed laws of ethics in research and issued codes of practice that are widely available online.

Conclusion

Conducting research that is ethically acceptable is a requirement nowadays. Researchers must abide by specific ethical principles such as those of avoiding harm to participants, informing participants adequately, ensuring confidentiality and being honest. Codes of research ethics, as well as ethics committees, work towards protecting research participants from any kind of harm within the context of research. Researchers are also protected from any possible legal action against them should the research participants consider that participating in a study may have caused them physical or psychological harm. Breast cancer, like other chronic conditions, causes patients to be vulnerable research subjects who need to be protected more carefully by researchers. Given this, codes of research ethics and the work of ethics committees are even more important.

References

Arman M and Rehnsfeldt A (2003) The hidden suffering among breast cancer patients: A qualitative metasynthesis. *Qualitative Health Research* 13(4): 510–527.

Bell K (2014) The breast-cancer-ization of cancer survivorship: Implications for experiences of the disease. *Social Sciences & Medicine* 110: 54–63.

Burke NJ, Villero O and Guerra C (2012) Passing through: Meanings of survivorship and support among Filipinas with breast cancer. *Qualitative Health Research* 22(2): 189–198.

Bower JE, Ganz PA, Desmond KA, Rowland JH, Meyerowitz BE and Belin TR (2000) Fatigue in breast cancer survivors: Occurrence, correlates, and impact on quality of life. *Journal of Clinical Oncology* 18(4): 743–753.

Bryman A (2001) Social research methods. Oxford: Oxford University Press.

Campbell-Crofts S, Field J and Fetherstonhaugh D (2013) Ethical considerations for nurses undertaking research with a potential vulnerable population with chronic kidney disease. *Renal Society of Australasia Journal* 9(2): 74–79.

Ching SSY, Martison IM and Wong TKS (2012) Meaning making: Psychological adjustment to breast cancer by Chinese women. *Qualitative Health Research* 22(2): 250–262.

Davey MP, Nino A, Kissil K and Ingram M (2012) African American parents' experiences navigating breast cancer while caring for their children. *Qualitative Health Research* 22(9): 1260–1270.

Jassin GA and Whitford DL (2014) Understanding the experiences and quality of life issues of Bahraini women with breast cancer. *Social Science & Medicine* 107: 189–195.

Kaiser K (2008) The meaning of the survivor identity for women with breast cancer. *Social Science & Medicine* 67: 79–87.

Klawiter M (2004) Breast cancer in two regimes: The impact of social movements on illness experience. *Sociology of Health & Illness* 26(6): 845–874.

Mackenzie CR (2014) "It is hard for mums to put themselves first": how mother diagnosed with breast cancer manage the sociological boundaries between paid work, family and caring for the self. *Social Science & Medicine* 117: 96–106.

Pistrang N, Barker C and Rutter C (1997) Social support as conversation: Analyzing breast cancer patients' interactions with their partners. *Social Science & Medicine* 45(5): 773–782.

Sarenmalm EK, Thoren-Jonsson A, Gaston-Johanson F and Ohlen J (2009) Making sense of living under the shadow of death: Adjusting to a recurrent breast cancer illness. *Qualitative Health Research* 19(8): 1116–1130.

Takahashi M and Kai I (2005) Sexuality and breast cancer treatment: Changes and coping strategies among Japanese survivors. *Social Science & Medicine* 61: 1278–1290.

Thomas-MacLean R (2004) Understanding breast cancer stories via Frank's narrative types. *Social Science & Medicine* 58: 1647–1657.

Whitehead S and Laveille K (2009) Older breast cancer survivors' views and preferences for physical activity. *Qualitative Health Research* 19(7): 894–906.

Wolf BM (2014) Do families cope communally with breast cancer, or is it just talk? *Qualitative Health Research* 25(3): 320–335.

Index